A BIBLICAL STUDY OF THE CATECHISM OF THE CATHOLIC CHURCH

Bible Answers to the Most Frequently Asked Questions about Catholic Beliefs and Practices

Jonathan Logan Carl

I am so thankful to God for His free gift of salvation in Jesus!

Ephesians 2:8–9 "For by grace you have been saved through faith. And this is not your own doing; it is the gift of God, not a result of works, so that no one may boast." (ESV)

I love and am so grateful for my amazing wife Brittney and her loving, tireless support.

Together we are blessed with some amazing daughters in Sophia, Lydia, Alia, and Mia! Our church family at South Fork has been so incredible in their encouragement :)

Thank you all for putting up with my many hours of studying & writing for this work!

FREE DOWNLOADS

Resources (articles, blogs, ebooks, handouts, powerpoints, etc.) and helpful study videos available at:

www.TrustworthyWord.com

or

www.Catholic.blog

CONTENTS

WELCOME!

Do you have questions about Catholic beliefs and practices? Would you like more information or a refresher on *The Catechism of the Catholic Church*? Whether you are Catholic, considering Catholicism, or just curious to understand the Catholic Church better, this Bible study will be a great help to you.

This work simply presents portions of the Catholic Catechism with relevant Bible verses and introspective questions to consider. This book will help you on your journey to consider the beliefs and practices of the Roman Catholic Church and examine for yourself, through tough questions, whether *The Catechism of the Catholic Church* is biblically valid and trustworthy.

The Catechism of the Catholic Church is a substantial document of significant history and tradition. If you have yet to read it, I encourage you to read it in its entirety. This guide should be a helpful start and reference! As you consider the "essential and fundamental contents of Catholic doctrine" (CCC, 11), I hope you will be like the Bereans of Acts 17:11 who always put the Bible first to test what they were learning.

The Bereans are described as "noble" after hearing the teaching of the Apostle Paul for two reasons:

1) getting into the Bible with "eagerness"

2) testing the teaching of the Apostle Paul in light of Scriptures to verify his truthfulness

Similarly, may we evaluate what we see in *The Catechism of the Catholic Church* in the light of the Bible to "see if these things were so."

Acts 17:11 "Now these Jews were more noble than those in Thessalonica; they received the word with all eagerness, examining the Scriptures daily to see if these things were so." (ESV)

A 3 Part Approach: Here is the approach you will find to this Bible study.

1) Interesting highlights and quotes - Due to the massive volume of writings in *The Catechism of the Catholic Church,* I have picked quotes from the text that I think you will find most useful and fascinating.

2) Relevant Scriptures - Likewise, I selected passages of Scripture that I thought particularly helpful in evaluating and understanding the Catholic teachings. Both *The Catechism of the Catholic Church* and the Bible passages should be considered in their original context and setting. There are many more possible Catholic teachings and Biblical passages to consider but I hope this is a helpful start to your studies.

3) Helpful Questions - I have chosen not to insert opinions and assertions but instead propose tough questions that help us to think critically for ourselves about what we are reading.

My end goal and hope is that we all follow God's directive to us in 2 Corinthians 13:5 to "Examine yourselves, to see whether you are in the faith. Test yourselves. Or do you not realize this about yourselves, that Jesus Christ is in you?—unless indeed you fail to meet the test!" (ESV). *May we all have the joy of an eternity in the presence of Jesus!*

Jesus was clear in stating that "Truly, truly, I say to you, unless one is born again he cannot see the kingdom of God." (John 3:3 ESV). If you haven't been born again into a personal trust in the Lordship of Christ, let me invite you to consider the below resources full of Scripture to help you on your journey to Jesus:

"How Can I Become a Christian?"
·www.trustworthyword.com/how-can-i-become-a-christian

"How Can I Be Sure I'm a Christian?"
·www.trustworthyword.com/how-can-i-be-sure-im-a-christian

"Evidence for Jesus"
·www.trustworthyword.com/evidence-for-jesus

Thanks for joining me on this journey! Please feel free to share this resource and discover more free Bible studies at: www.TrustworthyWord.com or www.Catholic.blog
In Christ, Dr. Jonathan Carl

1 Thessalonians 5:21 "test everything; hold fast what is good." (ESV)

CCC = The Catechism of the Catholic Church and the # is the Paragraph Referenced
ESV = The English Standard Version of the Bible

WHAT IS THE CATECHISM OF THE CATHOLIC CHURCH?

Passages of The Catechism of the Catholic Church to Consider:

- **"essential and fundamental contents of Catholic doctrine" (CCC, 11)**
- "I today order by virtue of my Apostolic Authority, is a statement of the Church's faith and of catholic doctrine, attested to or illumined by Sacred Scripture, the Apostolic Tradition, and the Church's Magesterium. **I declare it to be a sure norm for teaching the faith and thus a valid and legitimate instrument for ecclesial communion." (CCC, *Fidei Depositum*, Pope John Paul)**
- **"The presentation of doctrine must be biblical" (CCC, *Fidei Depositum*, Pope John Paul)**
- **"useful reading for all other Christian faithful" (CCC, 12)**
- **"For a deeper understanding of such passages, the reader should refer to the Scriptural texts themselves. Such Biblical references are a valuable working-tool in catechesis" (CCC, 19)**
- "It must be sound doctrine" (CCC, *Fidei Depositum*, Pope John Paul)
- "I beseech the Blessed Virgin Mary, Mother of the Incarnate Word and Mother of the Church, to support with her powerful

1

intercession the catechetical work of the entire Church on every level" (CCC, *Fidei Depositum*, Pope John Paul)
- "Catechesis is an education in the faith" (CCC, 4)
- "St. Cyril of Jerusalem and St. John Chrysostom, St. Ambrose and St. Augustine, and many other Fathers wrote catechetical works that remain models for us" (CCC, 8)

Scriptures to Consider:

- Deuteronomy 4.1–2 "And now, O Israel, listen to the statutes and the rules that I am teaching you, and do them, that you may live, and go in and take possession of the land that the LORD, the God of your fathers, is giving you. 2 **You shall not add to the word that I command you, nor take from it**, that you may keep the commandments of the LORD your God that I command you." (ESV)
- Deuteronomy 18:20–22 "But the prophet who presumes to speak a word in my name that I have not commanded him to speak, or who speaks in the name of other gods, that same prophet shall die. '[21] And if you say in your heart, 'How may we know the word that the LORD has not spoken?'—[22] when a prophet speaks in the name of the LORD, if the word does not come to pass or come true, that is a word that the LORD has not spoken; the prophet has spoken it presumptuously. You need not be afraid of him." (ESV)
- Proverbs 30:5–6 "Every word of God proves true; he is a shield to those who take refuge in him. Do not add to his words, lest he rebuke you and you be found a liar." (ESV)
- 2 John 9 "Everyone who goes on ahead and does not abide in the teaching of Christ, does not have God. Whoever abides in the teaching has both the Father and the Son." (ESV)
- Matthew 7:15–20 "Beware of false prophets, who come to you in sheep's clothing but inwardly are ravenous wolves. [16] You will recognize them by their fruits. Are grapes gathered from thornbushes, or figs from thistles? [17] So, every healthy tree

bears good fruit, but the diseased tree bears bad fruit. [18] A healthy tree cannot bear bad fruit, nor can a diseased tree bear good fruit. [19] Every tree that does not bear good fruit is cut down and thrown into the fire. [20] Thus you will recognize them by their fruits." (ESV)

- 2 Peter 2:1–3 "But false prophets also arose among the people, just as there will be false teachers among you, who will secretly bring in destructive heresies, even denying the Master who bought them, bringing upon themselves swift destruction. [2] And many will follow their sensuality, and because of them the way of truth will be blasphemed. [3] And in their greed they will exploit you with false words. Their condemnation from long ago is not idle, and their destruction is not asleep." (ESV)
- Revelation 22:18–19 "I warn everyone who hears the words of the prophecy of this book: if anyone adds to them, God will add to him the plagues described in this book, [19] and if anyone takes away from the words of the book of this prophecy, God will take away his share in the tree of life and in the holy city, which are described in this book." (ESV)
- John 14:26 "But **the Helper, the Holy Spirit**, whom the Father will send in my name, **he will teach you all things** and bring to your remembrance all that I have said to you." (ESV)

Questions to Consider:

- **Does the *Catechism of the Catholic Church* go beyond the teachings of Jesus? Is it biblical?**
- Why is there a need for tradition and the church authority in addition to the Bible?
- Why is there such a gap in time (350 years) between some of the early church writings that correspond to the claims of the catechism authority?
- Why are there so many internal inconsistencies in the *Catechism of the Catholic Church*? (note: see chapter towards the end that specifically addresses this concern)

- Why do some doctrines of the *Catechism of the Catholic Church* (purgatory, indulgences, etc.) validated later on in church history and mostly by tradition with little Scripture?
- Does the Catechism reference Scriptures within their contextual meaning? Have you ever checked the footnote references in the Catechism to be sure?
- Why are the Catechisms and Tradition of the Catholic Church allowed to change or be added to?
- Why does the Pope pray to the dead (Mary) for her prayers for the work of the Catechism? Is not talking to the dead directly called "necromancy"? Is it biblical?
- **What does John 14:26 say about who we access directly and primarily for help in teaching?**

HOW DO WE KNOW GOD?

Passages of The Catechism of the Catholic Church to Consider:

- "the Church is expressing her confidence in the possibility of speaking about him to all men and with all men" (CCC, 39)
- "the apostolic preaching, which is expressed in a special way in the inspired books, was to be preserved in a continuous line of succession until the end of time" (CCC, 77)
- **"this living transmission**, accomplished in the Holy Spirit, **is called Tradition**, since it is distinct from Sacred Scripture, though closely connected to it. Through Tradition, 'the Church, in her doctrine, life, and worship perpetuates and transmits to every generation all that she herself is, all that she believes" (CCC, 78)
- "The Father's self-communication made through his Word in the Holy Spirit, remains present and active in the Church" (CCC 79)

Scriptures to Consider:

- Matthew 28:19-20 "Go therefore and make disciples of all nations, baptizing them in the name of the Father and of the Son and of the Holy Spirit, teaching them to observe all that I have commanded you. And behold, I am with you always, to the end of the age." (ESV)
- Deuteronomy 6:6-7 "And these words that I command you

today shall be on your heart. 7 You shall teach them diligently to your children, and shall talk of them when you sit in your house, and when you walk by the way, and when you lie down, and when you rise." (ESV)

- **Mark 7:8–9 "You leave the commandment of God and hold to the tradition of men." And he said to them, "You have a fine way of rejecting the commandment of God in order to establish your tradition!"** (ESV)
- Psalm 19:7"The law of the Lord is perfect, reviving the soul; the testimony of the Lord is sure, making wise the simple" (ESV)
- Psalm 119:130 "The unfolding of your words gives light; it imparts understanding to the simple." (ESV)
- 2 Timothy 3:14-15 "But as for you, continue in what you have learned and have firmly believed, knowing from whom you learned it and how from childhood you have been acquainted with the **sacred writings, which are able to make you wise for salvation** through faith in Christ Jesus." (ESV)
- 2 Peter 3:16 "There are some things in them that are hard to understand, which the ignorant and unstable twist to their own destruction, as they do the other Scriptures" (ESV)
- 1 Peter 2:14 "The natural person does not accept the things of the Spirit of God, for they are folly to him, and he is not able to understand them because they are spiritually discerned." (ESV)
- **2 Timothy 2:15 "Do your best to present yourself to God as one approved, a worker who has no need to be ashamed, rightly handling the word of truth."** (ESV)
- John 10:14–16 "I am the good shepherd. I know my own and **my own know me**, [15] just as the Father knows me and I know the Father; and I lay down my life for the sheep. [16] And I have other sheep that are not of this fold. I must bring them also, and **they will listen to my voice**. So there will be one flock, one shepherd." (ESV)
- John 10:27–28 "My sheep hear my voice, and I know them, and they follow me. [28] I give them eternal life, and they will never perish, and no one will snatch them out of my hand." (ESV)

- Acts 17:11 "Now these Jews were more noble than those in Thessalonica; they received the word with all eagerness, examining the Scriptures daily to see if these things were so." (ESV)

Questions to Consider:

- Who is called to speak and teach authoritatively about Jesus?
- What is the role of the family in teaching about God?
- **Does the Bible give more encouragement (positive) about tradition or more warnings (negative) about traditions?**
- **NEGATIVE** - Matthew 15:1–9 "Then Pharisees and scribes came to Jesus from Jerusalem and said, [2] "Why do your disciples **break the tradition of the elders**? For they do not wash their hands when they eat." [3] He answered them, "**And why do you break the commandment of God for the sake of your tradition?** [4] For God commanded, 'Honor your father and your mother, 'and, 'Whoever reviles father or mother must surely die. '[5] But you say, 'If anyone tells his father or his mother, "What you would have gained from me is given to God," [6] he need not honor his father. 'So **for the sake of your tradition you have made void the word of God**. [7] You hypocrites! Well did Isaiah prophesy of you, when he said: [8] "'This people honors me with their lips, but their heart is far from me; [9] in vain do they worship me, teaching as doctrines the commandments of men.'" (ESV)
- **NEGATIVE** - Mark 7:1–13 "Now when the Pharisees gathered to him, with some of the scribes who had come from Jerusalem, [2] they saw that some of his disciples ate with hands that were defiled, that is, unwashed. [3] (For the Pharisees and all the Jews do not eat unless they wash their hands properly, **holding to the tradition of the elders**, [4] and when they come from the market-place, they do not eat unless they wash. And there are many other traditions that they observe, such as the washing of cups and pots and copper vessels and dining couches.) [5] And the Pharisees and the scribes asked him, "Why do **your disciples not walk according to the tradition of the elders**, but eat with defiled hands?" [6] And he said to them, "Well did Isaiah prophesy of you hypocrites, as it is written, "'This people honors me with their lips, but their heart is far from me; [7] **in vain do they worship me, teaching as doctrines**

the commandments of men.' [8] **You leave the commandment of God and hold to the tradition of men.**" [9] And he said to them, "You have a fine way of r**ejecting the commandment of God in order to establish your tradition!** [10] For Moses said, 'Honor your father and your mother'; and, 'Whoever reviles father or mother must surely die. '[11] But you say, 'If a man tells his father or his mother, "Whatever you would have gained from me is Corban '"(that is, given to God)—[12] then you no longer permit him to do anything for his father or mother, [13] **thus making void the word of God by your tradition that you have handed down. And many such things you do.**" (ESV)

- **POSITIVE** - 1 Corinthians 11:2 "Now I commend you because you remember me in everything and **maintain the traditions even as I delivered them to you.** (ESV)
- **NEGATIVE** - Galatians 1:13–16 "For you have heard of my former life in Judaism, how I persecuted the church of God violently and tried to destroy it. [14] And I was advancing in Judaism beyond many of my own age among my people, **so extremely zealous was I for the traditions** of my fathers." (ESV)
- **NEGATIVE** - Colossians 2:8 **"See to it that no one takes you captive by philosophy and empty deceit, according to human tradition**, according to the elemental spirits of the world, and not according to Christ." (ESV)
- **POSITIVE** - 2 Thessalonians 2:9–15 "But we ought always to give thanks to God for you, brothers beloved by the Lord, because God chose you as the firstfruits to be saved, through sanctification by the Spirit and **belief in the truth**. [14] To this he called you through our gospel, so that you may obtain the glory of our Lord Jesus Christ. [15] So then, brothers, stand firm and **hold to the traditions that you were taught by us, either by our spoken word or by our letter.**" (ESV)
- **POSITIVE** - 2 Thessalonians 3:6 "Now we command you, brothers, in the name of our Lord Jesus Christ, that you keep away from any brother who is walking in idleness and **not in accord with the tradition that you received from us**." (ESV)
- How does Psalm 119 describe the Bible?
- Are the writings and teachings of man (devotions, traditions, etc.) necessary for understanding how we know God through salvation?
- **What does 2 Timothy 3:14-15 say about salvation?**

8

- What is the best way to know and follow Jesus? Can we interact with Him directly?
- Read Acts 17:11. Why are the Bereans praised for testing the teaching of Paul? Why didn't they just presume what he said was true?

HOW DO WE KNOW TRUTH?

Passages of The Catechism of the Catholic Church to Consider:

- "'Sacred Tradition and Sacred Scripture, then, are bound closely together and **communicate one with the other**. For both of them, flowing out front he same divine well-spring, come together in some fashion to form one thing and move towards the same goal.' Each of them makes present and fruitful in the Church the mystery of Christ, who promised to remain with his own 'always, to the close of the age'" (CCC 80)
- **"As a result the Church, to whom the transmission and interpretation of Revelation is entrusted, 'does not derive her certainty about all revealed truths from the holy Scriptures alone. Both Scripture and Tradition must be accepted and honored with equal sentiments of devotion and reverence" (CCC 82)**
- "to the Church belongs the right always and everywhere to announce moral principles, including those pertaining to the social order, and to make judgments on any human affairs" (CCC 2032)
- "The Roman Pontiff and the bishops are 'authentic teachers, that is, teachers endowed with the authority of Christ, who preach the faith to be believed and put into practice" (CCC 2034)

Scriptures to Consider:

- 1 Timothy 6:3–5 "If anyone teaches **a different doctrine and does not agree with the sound words of our Lord Jesus Christ** and the teaching that accords with godliness, [4] he is puffed up with conceit and understands nothing. He has an unhealthy craving for controversy and for quarrels about words, which produce envy, dissension, slander, evil suspicions, [5] and constant friction among people who are depraved in mind and deprived of the truth, imagining that godliness is a means of gain." (ESV)
- 2 Timothy 3:16–17 **"All Scripture is breathed out by God** and profitable for teaching, for reproof, for correction, and for training in righteousness, [17] **that the man of God may be complete**, equipped for every good work." (ESV)
- **Acts 17:11 "Now these Jews were more noble than those in Thessalonica; they received the word with all eagerness, examining the Scriptures daily to see if these things were so."**
- 1 Corinthians 4:6 "I have applied all these things to myself and Apollos for your benefit, brothers, that you may **learn by us not to go beyond what is written**, that none of you may be puffed up in favor of one against another."
- 2 Timothy 4:2 "preach the word; be ready in season and out of season; reprove, rebuke, and exhort, with complete patience and teaching."
- **2 Corinthians 13:5 "Examine yourselves, to see whether you are in the faith. Test yourselves. Or do you not realize this about yourselves, that Jesus Christ is in you?—unless indeed you fail to meet the test!" (ESV)**
- Galatians 5:19–24 "Now the works of the flesh are evident: sexual immorality, impurity, sensuality, [20] idolatry, sorcery, enmity, strife, jealousy, fits of anger, rivalries, dissensions, divisions, [21] envy, drunkenness, orgies, and things like these. I warn you, as I warned you before, that those who do such things will not inherit the kingdom of God. [22] But the fruit

of the Spirit is love, joy, peace, patience, kindness, goodness, faithfulness, [23] gentleness, self-control; against such things there is no law. [24] And those who belong to Christ Jesus have crucified the flesh with its passions and desires." (ESV)

- 1 John 2:3–6 "And by this we know that we have come to know him, if we keep his commandments. [4] Whoever says "I know him" but does not keep his commandments is a liar, and the truth is not in him, [5] but whoever keeps his word, in him truly the love of God is perfected. By this we may know that we are in him: [6] whoever says he abides in him ought to walk in the same way in which he walked." (ESV)
- Matthew 13:18–23 "Hear then the parable of the sower: [19] When anyone hears the word of the kingdom and does not understand it, the evil one comes and snatches away what has been sown in his heart. This is what was sown along the path. [20] As for what was sown on rocky ground, this is the one who hears the word and immediately receives it with joy, [21] yet he has no root in himself, but endures for a while, and when tribulation or persecution arises on account of the word, immediately he falls away. [22] As for what was sown among thorns, this is the one who hears the word, but the cares of the world and the deceitfulness of riches choke the word, and it proves unfruitful. [23] As for what was sown on good soil, this is the one who hears the word and understands it. He indeed bears fruit and yields, in one case a hundredfold, in another sixty, and in another thirty." (ESV)
- Ephesians 3:16–17 "that according to the riches of his glory he may grant you to be strengthened with power through his Spirit in your inner being, [17] so that Christ may dwell in your hearts through faith—that you, being rooted and grounded in love" (ESV)
- Colossians 3:16 "Let the word of Christ dwell in you richly, teaching and admonishing one another in all wisdom, singing psalms and hymns and spiritual songs, with thankfulness in your hearts to God." (ESV)
- John 14:16–17 "And I will ask the Father, and he will give you

another Helper, to be with you forever, [17] even the Spirit of truth, whom the world cannot receive, because it neither sees him nor knows him. You know him, for he dwells with you and will be in you." (ESV)

Questions to Consider:

- Why does the Catechism claim a necessity for Scripture to be supported by Tradition?
- How do we know whose claims to authority are correct? How do we know if the claims of the Orthodox churches are superior to the Roman Catholic claims? What about Protestant traditions?
- Why is Tradition to be "accepted and honored with equal sentiments of devotion and reverence"?
- **How does 2 Timothy 3:16-17 describe the Bible?**
- Why is it so serious and dangerous to go beyond the teachings of God in the Bible?
- Why is there so much arrogance when talking through these differences?
- What does 2 Corinthians 13:5 say about salvation? How do we test ourselves according to Scripture?
- Would Galatians 5:19-24 be a good test, why?
- How would the book of 1 John help to test the genuineness of our faith?
- How does the parable of the sower help us to understand what salvation looks like? (Matthew 13:18–23)
- Why are conversations about our differences so important?
- How do we get prepared to explain our faith to others?
- **Who is our ultimate Helper in understanding truth according to John 14:16-17?**
- What other Bible passages would you add to this list? Why?

DOES CHURCH TRADITION CHANGE?

Does God's Revelation Continue?

Passages of The Catechism of the Catholic Church to Consider:

- **"In light of Tradition, these traditions can be retained, modified or even abandoned under the guidance of the Church's magisterium" (CCC 83)**
- "We believe all 'that which is contained in the word of God, written or handed down, **and which the Church proposes for belief** as divinely revealed" (CCC 182)

Scriptures to Consider:

- **Malachi 3:6 "For I the Lord do not change"**
- James 1:17 "Every good gift and every perfect gift is from above, coming down from the Father of lights, with whom there is no variation or shadow due to change."
- Numbers 23:19 "God is not man, that he should lie, or a son of man, that he should change his mind. Has he said, and will he not do it? Or has he spoken, and will he not fulfill it?"
- Revelation 22:18-20 "warn everyone who hears the words of the prophecy of this book: if anyone adds to them, God will add to him the plagues described in this book, 19 and if anyone takes away from the words of the book of this prophecy, God

will take away his share in the tree of life"

- Proverbs 30:5-6 "Every word of God proves true; he is a shield to those who take refuge in him. **Do not add to his words**, lest he rebuke you and you be found a liar."
- Deuteronomy 4:1–2 "And now, O Israel, listen to the statutes and the rules that I am teaching you, and do them, that you may live, and go in and take possession of the land that the LORD, the God of your fathers, is giving you. [2] You shall not add to the word that I command you, nor take from it, that you may keep the commandments of the LORD your God that I command you." (ESV)
- 2 John 9–10 "Everyone who goes on ahead and does not abide in the teaching of Christ, does not have God. Whoever abides in the teaching has both the Father and the Son. [10] If anyone comes to you and does not bring this teaching, do not receive him into your house or give him any greeting" (ESV)
- Jude 3–4 "I found it necessary to write appealing to you to contend for **the faith that was _once for all delivered to the saints_. [4]** For certain people have crept in unnoticed who long ago were designated for this condemnation, ungodly people, who **pervert the grace of our God**"
- Galatians 1:6–9 "I am astonished that you are so quickly deserting him who called you in the grace of Christ and are **turning to a different gospel**—[7] not that there is another one, but there are some who trouble you and want to distort the gospel of Christ. [8] But even if we or an angel from heaven should preach to you a gospel contrary to the one we preached to you, let him be accursed. [9] As we have said before, so now I say again: If anyone is preaching to you a gospel contrary to the one you received, let him be accursed." (ESV)
- 2 Peter 1:21 "For no prophecy was ever produced by the will of man, but **men spoke from God as they were carried along by the Holy Spirit**." (ESV)

Questions to Consider:

- Does God change with time? How does God reveal Himself to us specifically?
- **Since the Bible is complete and purposed to describe God to us, why does it need to be added to by Tradition if God does not change?**
- If Tradition is divinely inspired, why does it change with time and church leadership when the Bible does not? Why have parts been edited out and added in?
- Why would it be so serious and dangerous to add words, verses, or passages to the Bible?
- In what scenarios would it be necessary for the Catholic Church to add new revelation of Tradition?
- **How do we discern if a prophet or teacher is true or false? How do we recognize a "different gospel"?**
- Why does God give us so many warnings about false teachers?
- Is the Bible sufficient for our studies of truth?
- Where are the Bible and The Catechism of the Catholic Church similar? Different?

WHO CAN TEACH AUTHORITATIVELY?

Can Only Catholic Priests, Bishops, & Popes Interpret The Bible?

Passages of The Catechism of the Catholic Church to Consider:

- "It is clear therefore that, in the supremely wise arrangement of God, sacred Tradition, Sacred Scripture, and the Magisterium of the Church are so connected and associated that <u>one of them cannot stand without the others</u>. Working together each in its own way, under the action of the one Holy Spirit, they all contribute effectively to the salvation of souls." (CCC 95)
- "The task of giving an **authentic interpretation of the Word of God**, whether in its written form or the form of Tradition, has been **entrusted to the living, teaching office of the Church alone**" (CCC 85)
- **"The task of interpreting the Word of God authentically has been entrusted solely to the Magesterium of the Church, that is, to the Pope and to the bishops in communion with him." (CCC 100)**
- "It was by the apostolic Tradition that the Church discerned which writings are to be included in the list of the sacred books." (CCC 120)
- "Tobit, Judith…1 and 2 Maccabees…Wisdom, Sirach (Ecclesi-

asticus)...Baruch" (CCC 120)

- "Sacred Scripture is written principally in the Church's heart rather than in documents and records." (CCC 113)

Scriptures to Consider:

- 2 Timothy 3:16–17 "All Scripture is breathed out by God and profitable for teaching, for reproof, for correction, and for training in righteousness, [17] that the man of God may be complete, equipped for every good work." (ESV)
- 2 Timothy 3:15 "how from childhood you have been acquainted with the sacred writings, which are able to make you wise for salvation through faith in Christ Jesus."
- Psalm 19:7–14 "**The law of the LORD is perfect**, reviving the soul; the testimony of the LORD is sure, making wise the simple; [8] the precepts of the LORD are right, rejoicing the heart; the commandment of the LORD is pure, enlightening the eyes"
- John 10:27–30 "My sheep hear my voice, and I know them, and they follow me. [28] I give them eternal life, and they will never perish, and no one will snatch them out of my hand. [29] My Father, who has given them to me, is greater than all, and no one is able to snatch them out of the Father's hand. [30] I and the Father are one." (ESV)
- 1 Peter 2:5–9 "you yourselves like living stones are being built up as a spiritual house, to be a holy priesthood, to offer spiritual sacrifices acceptable to God through Jesus Christ. [6] For it stands in Scripture: 'Behold, I am laying in Zion a stone, a cornerstone chosen and precious, and whoever believes in him will not be put to shame." [7] So the honor is for you who believe, but for those who do not believe, "The stone that the builders rejected has become the cornerstone," [8] and "A stone of stumbling, and a rock of offense." They stumble because they disobey the word, as they were destined to do. [9] But you are a chosen race, a royal priesthood, a holy nation, a people for his own possession, that you may proclaim the excellen-

cies of him who called you out of darkness into his marvelous light." (ESV)

- 1 Timothy 2:5 "For there is one God, and there is one mediator between God and men, the man Christ Jesus"
- Hebrews 10:12 "But when Christ had offered for all time a single sacrifice for sins, he sat down at the right hand of God,"
- Hebrews 4:14–16 "Since then we have a great high priest who has passed through the heavens, Jesus, the Son of God, let us hold fast our confession. [15] For we do not have a high priest who is unable to sympathize with our weaknesses, but one who in every respect has been tempted as we are, yet without sin. [16] **Let us then with confidence draw near to the throne of grace, that we may receive mercy and find grace to help in time of need**." (ESV)
- 1 Corinthians 2:11–13 "For who knows a person's thoughts except the spirit of that person, which is in him? So also no one comprehends the thoughts of God except the Spirit of God. [12] Now we have received not the spirit of the world, but the Spirit who is from God, that we might understand the things freely given us by God. [13] And we impart this in words not taught by human wisdom but taught by the Spirit, interpreting spiritual truths to those who are spiritual." (ESV)
- John 14:26 "But the Helper, the Holy Spirit, whom the Father will send in my name, he will teach you all things and bring to your remembrance all that I have said to you."
- Ephesians 1:17–18 "that the God of our Lord Jesus Christ, the Father of glory, may give you the **Spirit of wisdom and of revelation in the knowledge of him**, [18] having the eyes of your hearts enlightened, that you may know what is the hope to which he has called you, what are the riches of his glorious inheritance in the saints" (ESV)
- John 16:13 "When the **Spirit of truth** comes, he will guide you into all the truth, for he will not speak on his own authority, but whatever he hears he will speak, and he will declare to you the things that are to come." (ESV)
- Jeremiah 17:9 "The heart is deceitful above all things, and

desperately sick; who can understand it" (ESV)

- Matthew 21:42 "Jesus said to them, "Have you never read in the Scriptures"
- 1 Timothy 4:13 "Until I come, devote yourself to the public reading of Scripture, to exhortation, to teaching." (ESV)
- Revelation 1:3 "Blessed is the one who reads aloud the words of this prophecy, and blessed are those who hear, and who keep what is written in it, for the time is near." (ESV)

Questions to Consider:

- If the Roman Catholic Church is has the exclusive claim to "authentic interpretation", does that mean Orthodox and Protestant Churches are invalid?
- **What does it mean to say that the Bible cannot stand without the Roman Catholic Tradition and Magisterium? Is that a biblical claim?**
- Who saves us? Jesus alone? A Church or Denomination?
- Who are Christians called to follow?
- **Are the biblical claims to authority based on faithfulness to God or the chronological/familial lineage?** What happened in the Bible if a King/Judge/Prophet was unfaithful to God's truth?
- Has the Catholic Church been faithful to God's truth and love over the past two millennia?
- Does the Holy Spirit indwell Churches or people? What is the task of the Holy Spirit? Who has the Holy Spirit?
- **Why do some of the more controversial Catholic teachings (indulgences, purgatory, penance, transubstantiation, baptismal regeneration, veneration of and prayer to Mary and the saints, etc.) come primarily from the Deuterocanon/ Apocrypha (i.e. books not usually found in Protestant Bibles) and Tradition?**
- What does it mean to say that "Sacred Scripture is written principally in the Church's heart rather than in documents and

records."? Are our hearts trustworthy?

- Why does Jesus and the New Testament give so much attention to reading the Bible?

WHAT IS A VALID CHURCH?

Is The Catholic Church The Only True Church?

Passages of The Catechism of the Catholic Church to Consider:

- **"The Church is the Temple of the Holy Spirit"** (CCC 809)
- **"This is the sole Church of Christ" (CCC 811)**
- "The sole Church of Christ [is that] which our Savior, after his Resurrection, entrusted to Peter's pastoral care, commissioning him and the other apostles to extend and rule it. ... This Church, constituted and organized as a society in the present world, subsists in (*subsistit in*) the Catholic Church, which is governed by the successor of Peter and by the bishops in communion with him." (CCC 816)
- **"For it is through Christ's Catholic Church alone, which is the universal hope toward salvation, that the fullness of the means of salvation can be obtained" (CCC 816)**

Scriptures to Consider:

- 1 Corinthians 6:19–20 "Or do you not know that your body is a temple of the Holy Spirit within you, whom you have from God? You are not your own, [20] for you were bought with a price. So glorify God in your body." (ESV)
- 1 Corinthians 3:16–17 "Do you not know that **you are God's**

temple and that God's Spirit dwells in you? [17] If anyone destroys God's temple, God will destroy him. For God's temple is holy, and you are that temple." (ESV)

- 2 Timothy 3:15 "the sacred writings, which are able to make you wise for salvation through faith in Christ Jesus." (ESV)
- 1 Thessalonians 5:9–10 "For God has not destined us for wrath, but to obtain salvation through our Lord Jesus Christ, [10] who died for us so that whether we are awake or asleep we might live with him." (ESV)
- Hebrews 10:24-25 "And let us consider how to stir up one another to love and good works, not neglecting to meet together, as is the habit of some, but encouraging one another, and all the more as you see the Day drawing near"
- Ephesians 1:22-23 "**the church, which is his body**"
- 1 Corinthians 12:20 "As it is, there are many parts, yet one body."
- 1 Corinthians 12:27-31 "Now **you are the body of Christ and individually members of it**.28 And God has appointed in the church first apostles, second prophets, third teachers, then miracles, then gifts of healing, helping, administrating, and various kinds of tongues. 29 Are all apostles? Are all prophets? Are all teachers? Do all work miracles? 30 Do all possess gifts of healing? Do all speak with tongues? Do all interpret? 31 But earnestly desire the higher gifts. And I will show you a still more excellent way."

Questions to Consider:

- Is God's Spirit constrained to a building or a denomination?
- What is a church? What is the purpose of a church?
- **Are all churches valid? What constitutes a true church?**
- **Does salvation come through a church or through Jesus?**
- How do we most accurately learn about Jesus?
- How do we ensure our faith is true?

WHAT IS SIN?

Do Different Sins Need Different Sacrifices?

Passages of The Catechism of the Catholic Church to Consider:

- **"The distinction between mortal and venial sin, already evident in Scripture, became part of the tradition of the Church. It is corroborated by human experience" (CCC 1854)**
- "Mortal sin destroys charity in the heart of man by a grave violation of God's law; it turns man away from God, who is his ultimate end and his beatitude by preferring and inferior good to him" (CCC 1855)
- "Venial sin allows charity to subsist, even though it offends and wounds it" (CCC 1855)
- "Mortal sin...necessitates a new initiative of God's mercy and a conversion of the heart which is normally accomplished within the sacrament of reconciliation" (CCC 1856)
- "Mortal sin is sin whose object is grave matter and which is also committed with full knowledge and deliberate consent" (CCC 1857)
- "Grave matter is specified by the Ten Commandments" (CCC 1858)
- **"Grave sin deprives us of communion with God and therefore makes us incapable of eternal life" (CCC 1472)**
- **"every sin, even venial, entails an unhealthy attachment to creatures, which must be purified here on earth, or after death in a state called Purgatory" (CCC 1472)**

- "this purification frees one from what is called the 'temporal punishment' of sin" (CCC 1472)

Scriptures to Consider:

- 1 John 2:16–17 "For all that is in the world—the desires of the flesh and the desires of the eyes and pride of life—is not from the Father but is from the world. [17] And the world is passing away along with its desires, but whoever does the will of God abides forever." (ESV)
- Galatians 2:16 "yet we know that a person is not justified by works of the law but through faith in Jesus Christ, so we also have believed in Christ Jesus, in order to be justified by faith in Christ and not by works of the law, because by works of the law no one will be justified." (ESV)
- Romans 3:19–20 "Now we know that whatever the law says it speaks to those who are under the law, so that every mouth may be stopped, and the whole world may be held accountable to God. [20] For by works of the law no human being will be justified in his sight, since through the law comes knowledge of sin." (ESV)
- Matthew 5:20 "For I tell you, unless your righteousness exceeds that of the scribes and Pharisees, you will never enter the kingdom of heaven." (ESV)
- Galatians 2:20–21 "I have been crucified with Christ. It is no longer I who live, but Christ who lives in me. And the life I now live in the flesh I live by faith in the Son of God, who loved me and gave himself for me. [21] I do not nullify the grace of God, for if righteousness were through the law, then Christ died for no purpose." (ESV)
- Mark 10:26–27 "And they were exceedingly astonished, and said to him, "Then who can be saved?" [27] Jesus looked at them and said, "With man it is impossible, but not with God. For all things are possible with God." (ESV)
- James 2:10 "For **whoever keeps the whole law but fails in one**

point has become guilty of all of it." (ESV)
- James 4:17 "So whoever knows the right thing to do and fails to do it, for him it is sin." (ESV)
- 1 John 1:9 "**If we confess our sins, he is faithful and just to forgive us our sins and to cleanse us from all unrighteousness.**" (ESV)

- Hebrews 7:27 "He has no need, like those high priests, to offer sacrifices daily, first for his own sins and then for those of the people, since **he did this once for all when he offered up himself.**" (ESV)
- Romans 8:1–2 "**There is therefore now no condemnation for those who are in Christ Jesus**. [2] For the law of the Spirit of life has set you free in Christ Jesus from the law of sin and death." (ESV)

Questions to Consider:
- **Is 1 John 2:16-17 distinguishing between different levels of sin or different ways in which we are tempted to sin?**
- Is tradition alone such a valid tool to determine whether someone goes to Heaven, Hell or Purgatory?
- Where does the Bible rank, compare, and evaluate the seriousness of sin?
- **What does James 2:10 mean? What does James 4:17 mean?**
- What is the purpose of the law according to Romans 3:19–20? Can fulfilling the law save us?
- Is it possible to fulfill the Ten Commandments? Who is the only one who has fulfilled the law?
- How can we obtain a righteousness that "exceeds the scribes and the Pharisees"?
- In the story of the rich young man (Mark 10:17-27), how did Jesus answer his question? Is it possible for man to save himself by fulfilling the Ten Commandments?
- **Does 1 John 1:9 say anything about different kinds of sins or different ways of obtaining forgiveness? How do we receive**

forgiveness? **Who do we confess to according to this verse?**
- Where does the Bible speak about purgatory? If purgatory exists, why would it exist if we are already forgiven "from all unrighteousness"?
- **What does Romans 8:1-2 mean?**

HOW CAN WE BE SAVED?

Is Salvation Alone Through The Catholic Church?

Passages of The Catechism of the Catholic Church to Consider:

- **"No one can have God as Father who does not have the Church as Mother" (CCC 181)**
- "It is the Church that believes first, and so bears, nourishes, and sustains my faith" (CCC 168)
- "we receive the life of faith through the Church, she is our mother: 'We believe **the Church as the mother of our new birth"** (CCC 169)
- "We believe all 'that which is contained in the word of God, written or handed down, and which the Church proposes for belief as divinely revealed" (CCC 182)
- **"For it is through Christ's Catholic Church alone, which is the universal hope toward salvation, that the fullness of the means of salvation can be obtained" (CCC 816)**
- "There is no offense, however serious, that the Church cannot forgive" (CCC 982)
- **"the Church possesses the power to forgive the sins** of the baptized and exercises it through bishops and priests normally in the sacrament of Penance" (CCC 986)
- "In the forgiveness of sins, both priests and sacraments are instruments through which our Lord Jesus Christ, the only au-

thor and liberal giver of salvation, wills to use in order to efface our sins and give us the grace of justification" (CCC 987)
- **"It is only within the faith of the Church that each of the faithful can believe" (CCC 1253)**
- **"Reconciliation with the Church is inseparable from reconciliation with God" (CCC 1445)**

Scriptures to Consider:

- John 14:6 "Jesus said to him, 'I am the way, and the truth, and the life. **No one comes to the Father except through me.**'" (ESV)
- Acts 4:12 "And there is salvation in no one else, for **there is no other name under heaven given among men by which we must be saved.**" (ESV)
- John 6:40 "For this is the will of my Father, that everyone who **looks on the Son and believes** in him should have eternal life, and I will raise him up on the last day." (ESV)
- 1 John 1:2–3 "the life was made manifest, and we have seen it, and testify to it and proclaim to you the eternal life, which was with the Father and was made manifest to us— [3] that which we have seen and heard we proclaim also to you, so that you too may have fellowship with us; and indeed our fellowship is with the Father and with his Son Jesus Christ." (ESV)
- 1 John 2:23 "No one who denies the Son has the Father. Whoever confesses the Son has the Father also." (ESV)
- Hebrews 12:2 "looking to Jesus, the founder and perfecter of our faith"
- 1 Peter 1:23 "since you have been *born again*, not of perishable seed but of imperishable, *through the living and abiding word of God*" (ESV)
- 2 Timothy 3:15 "from childhood you have been acquainted with the sacred writings, which are able to make you wise for salvation through faith in Christ Jesus." (ESV)

- 2 John 9–10 "Everyone who goes on ahead and does not abide in the teaching of Christ, does not have God. Whoever abides in the teaching has both the Father and the Son. [10] If anyone comes to you and does not bring this teaching, do not receive him into your house or give him any greeting" (ESV)
- Ephesians 4:32 "Be kind to one another, tenderhearted, forgiving one another, as God in Christ forgave you." (ESV)
- Acts 5:31 "God exalted him at his right hand as Leader and Savior, to give repentance to Israel and forgiveness of sins." (ESV)
- Luke 5:24 "But that you may know that **the Son of Man has authority on earth to forgive sins**"—he said to the man who was paralyzed—"I say to you, rise, pick up your bed and go home." (ESV)
- 1 John 1:9 "If we confess our sins, **he is faithful and just to forgive us our sins** and to cleanse us from all unrighteousness." (ESV)
- Romans 8:28–30 "And we know that for those who love God all things work together for good, for those who are called according to his purpose. [29] For those whom he foreknew he also predestined to be conformed to the image of his Son, in order that he might be the firstborn among many brothers. [30] And those whom he predestined he also called, and those whom he called he also justified, and those whom he justified he also glorified." (ESV)
- Romans 10:9–10 "because, **if you confess with your mouth that Jesus is Lord and believe in your heart that God raised him from the dead, you will be saved**. [10] For with the heart one believes and is justified, and with the mouth one confesses and is saved." (ESV)

Questions to Consider:

- Which Catechism quote stood out most to you? Why?
- Which Bible verse impacted you the most? Why?

- How do we have God as our Father? What does Jesus say in John 14:6? Why does He mention not the Church or Peter's priesthood and authority?
- How can we be born again? Have eternal life? Become a child of God?
- Who has the power to forgive sins according to Luke 5:24?
- How do we find forgiveness from sin? Does the Bible teach us that forgiveness comes through the church or directly through Jesus?
- **What does Romans 8:28-30 and 10:9-10 say about how salvation happens? Is salvation exclusive to belonging to a particular church or through Jesus being confessed as Lord and believed upon as resurrected?**

DOES GRACE COME THROUGH THE SACRAMENTS?

Do We Receive The Holy Spirit Through Sacraments?

Passages of The Catechism of the Catholic Church to Consider:

- "The whole liturgical life of the Church revolves around the Eucharistic sacrifice and sacraments....Baptism, Confirmation or Chrismation, Eucharist, Penance, Anointing of the Sick, Holy Orders, and Matrimony" (CCC 1113)
- **"Through the Church's sacraments, Christ communicates his Holy and sanctifying Spirit to the members of his Body." (CCC 739)**
- **"The communion of the sacraments...unite us to God" (CCC 951)**
- "Sacraments are 'powers that come forth' from the Body of Christ" (CCC 1116)
- "The ordained priesthood guarantees that it really is Christ who acts in the sacraments" (CCC 1120)
- "The three sacraments of Baptism, Confirmation, and Holy Orders confer, in addition to grace, a sacramental character or 'seal' by which the Christian shares in Christ's priesthood and is made a member of the Church" (CCC 1121)
- **"the sacraments confers the grace they signify. They are**

efficacious" (CCC 1127)

- **"The Church affirms that for believers the sacraments of the New Covenant are *necessary for salvation.*" (CCC 1129)**
- "The fruit of the sacramental life is that the Spirit of adoption makes the faithful the partakers in the divine nature by uniting them in loving union with the only Son, the Savior" (CCC 1129) [Council of Trent in 1547]
- "The New Law ... uses the sacraments to communicate grace to us" (CCC 1983)

Scriptures to Consider:

- **Ephesians 2:8–9 "For by grace you have been saved through faith. And this is not your own doing; it is the gift of God, [9] not a result of works, so that no one may boast." (ESV)**
- Galatians 2:16–21 "yet we know that a person is not justified by works of the law but through faith in Jesus Christ, so we also have believed in Christ Jesus, in order to be justified by faith in Christ and not by works of the law, because by works of the law no one will be justified. ... And the life I now live in the flesh I live by faith in the Son of God, who loved me and gave himself for me. [21] I do not nullify the grace of God, for if righteousness were through the law, then Christ died for no purpose." (ESV)
- Galatians 3:2–3 "Let me ask you only this: **Did you receive the Spirit by works of the law or by hearing with faith?** [3] Are you so foolish? Having begun by the Spirit, are you now being perfected by the flesh?" (ESV)
- Romans 5:15 "But the free gift is not like the trespass. For if many died through one man's trespass, much more have the grace of God and the free gift by the grace of that one man Jesus Christ abounded for many." (ESV)
- Jude 4 "For certain people have crept in unnoticed who long ago were designated for this condemnation, ungodly people, who pervert the grace of our God into sensuality and deny our

only Master and Lord, Jesus Christ." (ESV)

- Colossians 1:5–6 "you have heard before in the word of the truth, the gospel, [6] which has come to you, as indeed in the whole world it is bearing fruit and increasing—as it also does among you, since the day you heard it and understood the grace of God in truth" (ESV)
- Titus 2:11 "For the grace of God has appeared, bringing salvation for all people" (ESV)
- Romans 8:15 "For you did not receive the spirit of slavery to fall back into fear, but you have received the Spirit of adoption as sons, by whom we cry, 'Abba! Father!'" (ESV)
- Ephesians 1:5 "In love, he predestined us for adoption to himself as sons through Jesus Christ, according to the purpose of his will" (ESV)
- **John 1:12–13 "But to all who did receive him, who believed in his name, he gave the right to become children of God, [13] who were born, not of blood nor of the will of the flesh nor of the will of man, but of God." (ESV)**
- John 3:16 "For God so loved the world, that he gave his only Son, that whoever believes in him should not perish but have eternal life." (ESV)
- John 5:24 "Truly, truly, I say to you, whoever hears my word and believes him who sent me has eternal life. He does not come into judgment, but has passed from death to life." (ESV)
- John 6:47 "Truly, truly, I say to you, whoever believes has eternal life." (ESV)
- John 20:31 "but these are written so that you may believe that Jesus is the Christ, the Son of God, and that by believing you may have life in his name." (ESV)
- Acts 10:43 "To him all the prophets bear witness that everyone who believes in him receives forgiveness of sins through his name." (ESV)
- Acts 13:39 "by him everyone who believes is freed from everything from which you could not be freed by the law of Moses" (ESV)
- Acts 16:31 "And they said, 'Believe in the Lord Jesus, and you

will be saved, you and your household.'" (ESV)

Questions to Consider:

- If we are saved "by grace" and "it's not our doing" according to the Bible (Ephesians 2:8-9), then why do we need to be conferred grace by the sacraments (CCC 1127 and 1983)?
- **If we are "not justified by works" (Galatians 2:16) then why are the works of the sacraments "necessary for salvation" (CCC 1129)?**
- Why would the whole "life of the Church" (CCC 1113) revolve around rituals and ceremonies to receive grace? Does the New Testament say that's the primary task of the Church?
- **If Romans 8:15 and Ephesians 1:5 explain that we have already been adopted, then why do we need sacraments to "unite us to God" (CCC 951 and 1129)?**
- Is it biblical that the Holy Spirit is communicated to us through the sacraments (CCC 739)?
- Is it not true that the Bible describes all of the blessings of salvation as occurring at the point of faith? (See: John 1:12; 3:16; 5:24; 6:47; 20:31; Acts 10:43; 13:39; 16:31)

35

DOES SALVATION COME THROUGH CATHOLIC MASS?

Does Giving Money To Church Save Us?

Passages of The Catechism of the Catholic Church to Consider:

- "**the Church**, a pilgrim now on earth, **is necessary for salvation**" (CCC 846)
- **"They could not be saved who, knowing that the Catholic Church was founded as necessary by God through Christ, would refuse to enter it or to remain in it" (CCC 846)**
- "The liturgical celebration involves signs and symbols relating to creation (candles, water, fire), human life (washing, anointing, breaking bread), and the history of salvation (the rites of Passover)...**these cosmic elements, human rituals, and gestures of remembrance of God become bearers of the saving and sanctifying action of Christ" (CCC 1189)**
- "the faithful are bound to participate in the Mass" (CCC 2180)
- "the faithful are bound to participate in the Eucharist on days of obligation...those who deliberately fail in this obligation commit a grave sin" (CCC 2181)
- "the Church grants us the mercy of God which prevails over all our sins and is especially at work in us in the sacrament of reconciliation" (CCC 2040)

- "The first precept 'You shall attend Mass on Sundays and on holy days of obligation and rest from servile labor'" (CCC 2042)
- **"The second precept 'You shall confess your sins at least once per year' ensures preparation for the Eucharist by the reception of the sacrament of reconciliation, which continues Baptism's work of conversion and forgiveness" (CCC 2042)**
- "The third precept 'You shall receive the sacrament of the Eucharist at least during the Easter season.' guarantees as a minimum the reception of the Lord's Body and Blood in connection with the Paschal feasts, the origin and center of the Christian liturgy." (CCC 2042)
- "The fourth precept 'You shall observe the days of fasting and abstinence established by the Church' ensures the times of ascesis and penance which prepares us for the liturgical feasts and helps us to acquire mastery over our instincts and freedom of heart." (CCC 2043)
- "The first precept 'You shall help to provide for the needs of the Church' means that the faithful are obliged to assist with the material needs of the Church, each according to his own ability." (CCC 2043)
- **Tobit 4:11 "For alms deliver from all sin, and from death, and will not suffer the soul to go into darkness."**
- **Tobit 12:9 "For alms delivereth from death, and the same is that which purgeth away sins, and maketh to find mercy and life everlasting."**
- 2 Maccabees 12:43 "And making a gathering, he sent twelve thousand drachms of silver to Jerusalem **for sacrifice to be offered for the sins of the dead**, thinking well and religiously concerning the resurrection."

Scriptures to Consider:

- **Romans 10:9-10 "because, if you confess with your mouth that Jesus is Lord and believe in your heart that God raised** him from the dead, you will be saved. [10] For with the heart one believes and is justified, and with the mouth one confesses and is saved." (ESV)

- Ephesians 2:8–9 "For by grace you have been saved through faith. And this is not your own doing; it is the gift of God, [9] not a result of works, so that no one may boast." (ESV)
- Romans 10:17 "So faith comes from hearing, and hearing through the word of Christ." (ESV)
- 1 John 1:7 "But if we walk in the light, as he is in the light, we have fellowship with one another, and the blood of Jesus his Son cleanses us from all sin."
- Matthew 23:4 "They tie up heavy burdens, hard to bear, and lay them on people's shoulders, but they themselves are not willing to move them with their finger." (ESV)
- Luke 11:46 "And he said, "Woe to you lawyers also! For you load people with burdens hard to bear, and you yourselves do not touch the burdens with one of your fingers" (ESV)
- Acts 15:28–29 "For it has seemed good to the Holy Spirit and to us to lay on you no greater burden than these requirements: [29] that you abstain from what has been sacrificed to idols, and from blood, and from what has been strangled, and from sexual immorality. If you keep yourselves from these, you will do well. Farewell." (ESV)
- 1 Timothy 4:1–4 "Now the Spirit expressly says that in later times some will depart from the faith by devoting themselves to deceitful spirits and teachings of demons, [2] through the insincerity of liars whose consciences are seared, [3] who forbid marriage and require abstinence from foods that God created to be received with thanksgiving by those who believe and know the truth. [4] For everything created by God is good, and nothing is to be rejected if it is received with thanksgiving" (ESV)
- Philemon 8–9 "Accordingly, though I am bold enough in Christ to command you to do what is required, [9] yet for love's sake I prefer to appeal to you—I, Paul, an old man and now a prisoner also for Christ Jesus" (ESV)

- 2 Corinthians 9:5 "So I thought it necessary to urge the brothers to go on ahead to you and arrange in advance for the gift you have promised, so that it may be ready as a willing gift, not as an exaction." (ESV)
- **2 Corinthians 9:7 "Each one must give as he has decided in his heart, not reluctantly or under compulsion, for God loves a cheerful giver." (ESV)**

Questions to Consider:

- **Is there a Bible verse that you can find that says the Church is "necessary for salvation" (CCC 846)?**
- Why would the Catholic Church say that "they could not be saved" who "refuse to enter ... or to remain in" the Catholic Church? Do we lose our salvation because of not being a member of the Catholic Church?
- Why would the word "obligation" be used in so many ways with parts of the Mass?
- When is our "conversion" complete according to the Bible? At what point are we totally saved and forgiven according to Romans 10:9-10? Why would the Catholic Church add so many more requirements to salvation? How is that different than Acts 10:42-44?
- What are the warnings of Matthew 23:4 and Luke 11:46? Why does Paul warn Timothy about those who require "abstinence from foods" and "forbid marriage"? Do these warnings apply to the Catholic Church?
- **Why does Paul describe giving as something to do as a "willing gift" and "not under compulsion" (2 Corinthians 9:5-7)?** How is this different than being "obliged" (CCC 2043) and that "alms deliver from all sin" (Tobit 4:11) and that "alms delivereth from death" (Tobit 12:9)? Does this difference concern you? Why?
- **What do you think of 2 Maccabees 12:43?**

IS CATHOLIC BAPTISM NECESSARY FOR SALVATION?

Passages of The Catechism of the Catholic Church to Consider:

- "Those who belong to Christ through faith and Baptism must confess their baptismal faith before men" (CCC 14)
- "All who have been justified by faith in Baptism are incorporated into Christ." (CCC 818)
- "Baptism, the gate by which we enter into the Church." (CCC 950)
- **"Baptism is necessary for salvation for those who have not yet been reborn" (CCC 980)**
- "communicating forgiveness of sins in Baptism" (CCC 981)
- "The grace of the Holy Spirit has the power to justify us, that is, to cleanse us from our sins and to communicate to us 'the righteousness of God through faith in Jesus Christ' and through Baptism" (CCC 1987)
- **"Justification is conferred in Baptism, the sacrament of faith" (CCC 1992)**
- **"Baptism is the first and chief sacrament of forgiveness of sins because it unites us with Christ" (CCC 977)**
- "The faithful are **born anew** by Baptism" (CCC 1212)
- "Holy Baptism is the basis of the whole Christian life, the gateway to life in the Spirit" (CCC 1213)

- "Through Baptism we are **freed from sin and reborn** as sons of God" (CCC 1213)
- "Baptism is the sacrament of **regeneration** through water in the word" (CCC 1213)
- "This sacrament is also called the 'washing of regeneration and renewal by the Holy Spirit' for it signifies and actually brings about the birth of water and the Spirit without which no one 'can enter the Kingdom of God'" (CCC 1215)
- "exorcisms are pronounced over the candidate" (CCC 1237)
- "the baptismal water is consecrated by a prayer" (CCC 1238)
- "Baptism...signifies and actually brings about death to sin and entry into the life of the Most Holy Trinity through configuration to the Paschal mystery of Christ" (CCC 1239)
- "Baptism is performed in the most expressive way by triple immersion in the baptismal water. However from ancient times it has also been able to be conferred by pouring the water over the candidate's head" (CCC 1239)
- "The newly baptized is now, in the only Son, a child of God, entitled to say the prayer of the children of God: 'Our Father'" (CCC 1243)
- "Baptism is the source of that new life in Christ from which the entire Christian life springs forth" (CCC 1254)
- **"The Lord himself affirms that Baptism is necessary for salvation" (CCC 1257)**
- "Baptism is necessary for salvation for those whom the Gospel has been proclaimed and who had the possibility of asking for this sacrament" (CCC 1257)
- "**God has bound salvation to the sacrament of Baptism**, but he himself is not bound by his sacraments" (CCC 1257)
- "For catechumens who die before their Baptism, their explicit desire to receive it, together with repentance for their sins, and charity, assures them the salvation that they were not able to receive through the sacrament" (CCC 1259)
- **"By baptism all sins are forgiven" (CCC 1263)**
- **"Justified by faith in Baptism" (CCC 1271)**

- "Baptism seals the Christian with the indelible spiritual mark (character) of his belonging to Christ." (CCC 1272)

ARE INFANTS SAVED BY BAPTISM?

Passages of The Catechism of the Catholic Church to Consider:

- "Born with a fallen human nature and tainted by original sin, children have need of the new birth in Baptism to be freed from the power of darkness and brought into the realm of the freedom of the Children of God" (CCC 1250)
- "The Church and **the parents would deny a child the priceless grace of becoming a child of God were they not to confer Baptism shortly after birth**" (CCC 1250)
- "As regards children who have died with Baptism, the Church can only entrust them to the mercy of God, as she does in her funeral rites for them. ...**allow us to hope that there is a way of salvation for children who have died without Baptism**" (CCC 1261)
- "**with respect to children who have died without Baptism, the liturgy of the Church invites us to trust in God's mercy and to pray for their salvation**" (CCC 1283)

WHY IS EVERY CATHOLIC EXORCISED AT BAPTISM?

Passages of The Catechism of the Catholic Church to Consider:

- "When the Church asks publicly and authoritatively in the name of Jesus Christ that a person or object be protected against the power of the Evil One and withdrawn from his dominion, it is called exorcism" (CCC 1673)
- "Jesus performed exorcisms and from him the Church has received the power and office of exorcizing. In a simple form, **exorcism is performed at the celebration of Baptism.**" (CCC 1673)
- "The solemn exorcism, called a 'major exorcism, 'can be performed only by a priest and with the permission of the bishop. The priest must proceed with prudence, strictly observing the rules established by the Church." (1673)
- "Exorcism is directed at the expulsion of demons or to the liberation from demonic possession through he spiritual authority which Jesus entrusted to his Church." (1673)

Scriptures to Consider:

- **Titus 3:5 "he saved us, not because of works done by us in righteousness, but according to his own mercy, by the wash-**

ing of regeneration and renewal of the Holy Spirit" (ESV)

- John 3:5 "Jesus answered, 'Truly, truly, I say to you, unless one is born of water and the Spirit, he cannot enter the kingdom of God.'" (ESV)
- Ezekiel 36:25–27 "I will sprinkle clean water on you, and you shall be clean from all your uncleannesses, and from all your idols I will cleanse you. [26] And I will give you a new heart, and a new spirit I will put within you. And I will remove the heart of stone from your flesh and give you a heart of flesh. [27] And I will put my Spirit within you, and cause you to walk in my statutes and be careful to obey my rules." (ESV)
- Romans 6:3–4 "Do you not know that all of us who have been baptized into Christ Jesus were baptized into his death? [4] We were buried therefore with him by baptism into death, in order that, just as Christ was raised from the dead by the glory of the Father, we too might walk in newness of life." (ESV)
- 1 John 2:29 "If you know that he is righteous, you may be sure that everyone who practices righteousness has been born of him." (ESV)
- 1 John 3:9 "No one born of God makes a practice of sinning, for God's seed abides in him; and he cannot keep on sinning, because he has been born of God." (ESV)
- 1 John 4:7 "Beloved, let us love one another, for love is from God, and whoever loves has been born of God and knows God." (ESV)
- 1 John 5:1 "Everyone who believes that Jesus is the Christ has been born of God, and everyone who loves the Father loves whoever has been born of him." (ESV)
- 1 John 5:4 "For everyone who has been born of God overcomes the world. And this is the victory that has overcome the world —our faith." (ESV)
- 1 Corinthians 1:14 "I thank God that I baptized none of you except Crispus and Gaius"
- 1 Corinthians 1:17 "For Christ did not send me to baptize but to preach the gospel, and not with words of eloquent wisdom, lest the cross of Christ be emptied of its power."

- 1 Corinthians 15:1–8 "Now I would remind you, brothers, of the gospel I preached to you, which you received, in which you stand, [2] and by which you are being saved, if you hold fast to the word I preached to you—unless you believed in vain. [3] For I delivered to you as of first importance what I also received: that Christ died for our sins in accordance with the Scriptures, [4] that he was buried, that he was raised on the third day in accordance with the Scriptures, [5] and that he appeared to Cephas, then to the twelve. [6] Then he appeared to more than five hundred brothers at one time, most of whom are still alive, though some have fallen asleep. [7] Then he appeared to James, then to all the apostles. [8] Last of all, as to one untimely born, he appeared also to me." (ESV)
- 2 Samuel 12:21-23 "His servants asked him, "Why are you acting this way? While the child was alive, you fasted and wept, but now that the child is dead, you get up and eat!" 22 He answered, "While the child was still alive, I fasted and wept. I thought, 'Who knows? The LORD may be gracious to me and let the child live.' 23 But now that he is dead, why should I fast? Can I bring him back again? **I will go to him, but he will not return to me.**"
- Ecclesiastes 6:3-5 "I say that a stillborn child is better off than he." (ESV)
- Deuteronomy 1:39 "And as for your little ones, who you said would become a prey, and your children, who today have no knowledge of good or evil, they shall go in there. And to them I will give it, and they shall possess it." (ESV)
- Titus 2:11–12 "For the grace of God has appeared, bringing salvation for all people, [12] **training us to renounce ungodliness and worldly passions**, and to live self-controlled, upright, and godly lives in the present age" (ESV)
- Zechariah 3:2 "And the LORD said to Satan, "The LORD rebuke you, O Satan! The LORD who has chosen Jerusalem rebuke you! Is not this a brand plucked from the fire?" (ESV)
- Jude 9–10 "But when the archangel Michael, contending with the devil, was disputing about the body of Moses, he did not

presume to pronounce a blasphemous judgment, but said, **"The Lord rebuke you."** [10] But these people blaspheme all that they do not understand, and they are destroyed by all that they, like unreasoning animals, understand instinctively." (ESV)

- More scriptures on the death of babies and children: www.trustworthyword.com/what-does-the-bible-say-about-the-death-of-babies-children
- More scriptures on baptism: www.trustworthyword.com/what-does-the-bible-say-about-baptism
- An Ante-Nicene (early church fathers') historical approaches to spiritual warfare and exorcism: www.trustworthyword.com/sw-church-history (NOTE: very different from the much later (1614 A.D.) Catholic Church's *Rituale Romanum* approach to the demonic)

Questions to Consider:

- Why is Baptism such a big deal for Catholic doctrine? **What does it mean that Baptism isn't completed without penance, catechism, and the Eucharist? Is that seen in the Bible?**
- Is the "born of water" a reference to baptism in John 3:5? Or a reference to Ezekiel 36:25-27?
- Do the passages in 1 John speak about being born again by baptism? Or through belief? Love? Personal and relational knowledge of God? Evidenced by a changed life? In faith?
- Does Romans 6:3–4 describe being baptized into a church?
- **Why is the process of getting baptized &going through Catechism in the Catholic Church so lengthy compared to the instantaneous belief and baptisms seen in Acts 2:41, 8:36, 9:18, 16:33, 18:8, 19:5?**
- Is the consecration (blessing) of baptismal water in the Bible?
- Where is triple immersion in the Bible? Where is pouring over/infusion in the Bible?
- **Where does the Bible advocate for praying for someone's**

salvation after they already died?

- **If baptism is necessary for salvation, why would Paul say he was thankful that he only baptized two people at Corinth (1 Corinthians 1:14)?**
- If baptism is necessary for salvation, why would Paul say "Christ did not send me to baptize but to preach the gospel" (1 Corinthians 1:17)?
- Why Paul outlines the gospel in 1 Corinthians 15:1-8 why does he not mention baptism? What is his focus?
- What do these passages imply about the salvation of babies & children who die? 2 Samuel 12:21-23, Deuteronomy 1:39, Job 3:11-17, Ecclesiastes 6:3-5, & Jeremiah 19:4.
- Are baptismal exorcisms (casting out of Satan/demons) in the Bible? Why is exorcism performed as part of every Catholic Baptism?
- When exorcisms happen in the Bible what rules exist? Or is it a simple command in the authority and name of Jesus?
- Why does the Roman Catholic Church has such extensive rules and procedures for exorcism as encapsulated in *Rituale Romanum*?

6 TOUGH PASSAGES ON BAPTISM TO CONSIDER

The below passages are tough to understand and seem, on their own, to advocate for baptismal regeneration (that baptism saves). If we look more closely at them individual, we can see them more clearly and how they can be reconciled with the many Scriptures that explain that salvation comes through faith alone as a free gift of God's loving grace.

1) Does Acts 2:38 teach that baptism is necessary for salvation?

Acts 2:38, "And Peter said to them, 'Repent, and let each of you be baptized in the name of Jesus Christ for the forgiveness of your sins; and you shall receive the gift of the Holy Spirit.'"

- Could the best translation for "for" in this context be either "because of" or "in regard to" and not "in order to get"?
- Another important note is how some of the verbs and pronouns are different: some are singular and some are plural. Could this mean that "when you take into account the change in person and plurality, essentially what you have is 'You (plural) repent for the forgiveness of your (plural) sins, and let each one (singular) of you be baptized (singular).' Or, to put it in a more distinct way: 'You all repent for the forgiveness of all of your sins, and let each one of you be baptized.'" (for more

49

see: www.gotquestions.org/baptism-Acts-2-38.html)

2) Does Mark 16:16 teach that
baptism is necessary for salvation?

Mark 16:16 "Whoever believes and is baptized will be saved, but whoever does not believe will be condemned."
- An important translation note: "There is some question as to whether these verses were originally part of the Gospel of Mark or whether they were added later by a scribe. As a result, it is best not to base a key doctrine on anything from Mark 16:9-20, such as snake handling, unless it is also supported by other passages of Scripture."
- If this verse it to be included in Scripture, does it even describe the eternal status of those who "believe and have not been baptized"? We cannot for certain the opposite is true.
- What is the evidence of condemnation in this verse? Is it even connected to baptism?
- Does the Bible ever say that if one is not baptized they are not saved? What about the man on the cross next to Jesus who is never baptized, never goes to church, never takes Eucharist, and is never confirmed?
- What is required for salvation? Belief.
- More at: www.gotquestions.org/baptism-Mark-16-16.html

3) Does 1 Peter 3:21 teach that
baptism is necessary for salvation?

1 Peter 3:21 "Baptism, which corresponds to this, now saves you, not as a removal of dirt from the body but as an appeal to God for a good conscience, through the resurrection of Jesus Christ" (ESV)
- When Peter connects baptism to salvation, what is the root cause of the salvation? What does baptism represent? What does an "appeal to God" mean?

- Why does the Peter refer to the mechanical act of baptism ("removal of dirt")? It he pointing out that it isn't about the act itself, but about the inward appeal of belief and repentances?
- How did the waters of the flood "save" Noah and his family? How are the ark and baptism connected here (1 Peter 3:20)?
- Was Noah saved by his wisdom, obedience, skill, and hard work to build the ark? Or was he saved by his inwards trust and love of the Lord so that the God provided a rescue from the waters of judgment? Who shut the door of the ark (Genesis 7:16)?
- Are we saved by our wisdom, obedience, and diligence to get baptized? Or are we saved by our inward trust and love of the Lord in how He provided a rescue from the judgment of sin through His death and resurrection on the cross?
- See www.gotquestions.org/baptism-1Peter-3-21.html for more helpful thoughts.

4) Does John 3:5 teach that baptism is necessary for salvation?

John 3:5 "Jesus answered, 'Truly, truly, I say to you, unless one is born of water and the Spirit, he cannot enter the kingdom of God. (ESV)
- Why is the word "baptism" not explicitly used here but is used later in the chapter (John 3:22-30) at a different time and place?
- Why is water the symbol of cleansing throughout the Bible? (for examples see: Psalm 51:2,7; Ezekiel 36:25, John 13:10; 15:3; 1 Corinthians 6:11; Hebrews 10:22; Ephesians 5:26; Titus 3:5)
- How might this connect to the "living water" Jesus speaks to later in John? (John 4:10 & 7:37-39)
- How does this "water" cleanse us internally and eternally? (see Ezekiel 36:25-27 & Titus 3:5)
- Why is water used often to symbolize the Spirit's work in us?

(see Isaiah 44:3 & John 7:38-39)

- Was Nicodemus being rebuked for not understanding baptism or for not understanding these passages: Ezekiel 36:25-27 and Jeremiah 31:33.
- More insights here: www.gotquestions.org/baptism-John-3-5.html

5) Does Acts 22:16 teach that baptism is necessary for salvation?

Acts 22:16 "And now why do you wait? Rise and be baptized and wash away your sins, calling on his name."' (ESV)

- Did Paul believe before his baptism (Galatians 1:11-12)?
- Did Paul receive the Holy Spirit before his baptism? (Acts 9:17-18)
- A helpful translation note: "The Greek aorist participle, epikalesamenos, translated "calling on His name" refers either to action that is simultaneous with or before that of the main verb, "be baptized." Here Paul's calling on Christ's name for salvation preceded his water baptism. The participle may be translated "having called on His name" which makes more sense, as it would clearly indicate the order of the events."
- How does baptism externally portray the inward washing away of sin that happens at salvation? (1 Corinthians 6:11 and 1 Peter 3:21).
- When Paul shares his testimony of conversion with King Agrippa (Acts 26:12-18), why does He focus on meeting Jesus on the road to Damascus and not on his encounter with Ananias (Acts 9:10-17) and baptism?
- For further study, checkout: www.gotquestions.org/baptism-Acts-22-16.html

6) Does Galatians 3:27 teach that baptism is necessary for salvation?

Galatians 3:27 "For as many of you as were baptized into Christ have put on Christ." (ESV)

- Why is Paul writing this letter to the Galatians according to Galatians 1:6-10?
- What does he mean that we are "not justified by the works of the law but by faith in Christ" (Galatians 2:16) and that "you are all sons of God through faith in Christ Jesus" (Galatians 3:26)?
- Is this passage even talking about baptism into water? Or is it talking about union with Christ through the baptism of the Holy Spirit at the point of faith? What does Romans 8:9 say is the principal difference between believers and non-believers?
- How is Jesus the one "who baptizes with the Holy Spirit" (John 1:33-34)?
- What does it mean to be "sealed with the Holy Spirit of promise" (Ephesians 1:13-14)?
- More info on this passage here: www.gotquestions.org/baptism-Galatians-3-27.html

IS CATHOLIC CONFIRMATION NECESSARY FOR SALVATION?

Does Catholic Confirmation Confer The Holy Spirit?

Passages of The Catechism of the Catholic Church to Consider:

- **"the sacrament of Confirmation is necessary for the completion of baptismal grace" (CCC 1285)**
- "the apostles, in fulfillment of Christ's will, imparted to the newly baptized by the laying on of hands the gift of the Spirit that completes the grace of Baptism" (CCC 1288)
- "The imposition of hands is rightly recognized by the Catholic tradition as the origin of the sacrament of Confirmation, which in a certain way perpetuates the grace of Pentecost in the Church." (CCC 1288)
- "The term confirmation suggests that this sacrament both confirms baptism and strengthens baptismal grace" (CCC 1289)
- "the effect of the sacrament of Confirmation is the **special outpouring of the Holy Spirit** at once granted to the apostles on the day of Pentecost" (CCC 1302)

- "Confirmation brings an increase and deepening of the baptismal grace" (CCC 1303)
- "Confirmation ... roots us more deeply in the divine filiation which makes us cry, 'Abba! Father!'" (CCC 1303)
- **"Confirmation ... unites us more firmly to Christ" (CCC 1303)**
- **"Confirmation ... increases the gifts of the Holy Spirit" (CCC 1303)**
- **"Baptism which it completes" (CCC 1304)**
- "without Confirmation and Eucharist, Baptism is certainly valid and efficacious, but **Christian initiation remains incomplete**" (CCC 1306)
- "One should receive the sacrament of Penance in order to be cleansed for the gift of the Holy Spirit" (CCC 1310)
- "in danger of death children should be confirmed even if they have not yet attained the age of discretion" (CCC 1307)
- "If a Christian is in danger of death, any priest can give him Confirmation. Indeed the Church desires that none of her children, even the youngest, should depart this world without having been perfected by the Holy Spirit with the gift of Christ's fullness." (CCC 1314)
- **"Confirmation perfects Baptismal grace; it is the sacrament which gives the Holy Spirit" (CCC 1316)**

Scriptures to Consider:

- 1 Corinthians 12:13 "For in one Spirit we were all baptized into one body—Jews or Greeks, slaves or free—and all were made to drink of one Spirit." (ESV)
- 2 Corinthians 5:17 "Therefore, if anyone is in Christ, he is a new creation. The old has passed away; behold, the new has come." (ESV)
- Acts 8:14–17 "Now when the apostles at Jerusalem heard that Samaria had received the word of God, they sent to them Peter and John, [15] who came down and prayed for them that they might receive the Holy Spirit, [16] for he had not yet fallen on

any of them, but they had only been baptized in the name of the Lord Jesus. [17] Then they laid their hands on them and they received the Holy Spirit." (ESV)

- Acts 8:18–24 "Now when Simon saw that the Spirit was given through the laying on of the apostles' hands, he offered them money, [19] saying, 'Give me this power also, so that anyone on whom I lay my hands may receive the Holy Spirit.' [20] But Peter said to him, 'May your silver perish with you, because you thought you could obtain the gift of God with money! [21] You have neither part nor lot in this matter, for your heart is not right before God. [22] Repent, therefore, of this wickedness of yours, and pray to the Lord that, if possible, the intent of your heart may be forgiven you. [23] For I see that you are in the gall of bitterness and in the bond of iniquity.' [24] And Simon answered, 'Pray for me to the Lord, that nothing of what you have said may come upon me.'" (ESV)

- Acts 19:4–6 "And Paul said, 'John baptized with the baptism of repentance, telling the people to believe in the one who was to come after him, that is, Jesus." [5] On hearing this, they were baptized in the name of the Lord Jesus. [6] And when Paul had laid his hands on them, the Holy Spirit came on them, and they began speaking in tongues and prophesying.'" (ESV)

- **Ephesians 1:13–14 "In him you also, when you heard the word of truth, the gospel of your salvation, and believed in him, were sealed with the promised Holy Spirit, [14] who is the guarantee of our inheritance until we acquire possession of it, to the praise of his glory." (ESV)**

- Romans 8:9 "You, however, are not in the flesh but in the Spirit, if in fact the Spirit of God dwells in you. Anyone who does not have the Spirit of Christ does not belong to him." (ESV)

- **Romans 8:38–39 "For I am sure that neither death nor life, nor angels nor rulers, nor things present nor things to come, nor powers, [39] nor height nor depth, nor anything else in all creation, will be able to separate us from the love of God in Christ Jesus our Lord." (ESV)**

- John 3:5–8 "Jesus answered, 'Truly, truly, I say to you, unless one is born of water and the Spirit, he cannot enter the kingdom of God. [6] That which is born of the flesh is flesh, and that which is born of the Spirit is spirit. [7] Do not marvel that I said to you, 'You must be born again. '[8] The wind blows where it wishes, and you hear its sound, but you do not know where it comes from or where it goes. So it is with everyone who is born of the Spirit.'" (ESV)
- 1 Corinthians 6:19 "Or do you not know that your body is a temple of the Holy Spirit within you, whom you have from God?" (ESV)

Questions to Consider:

- If someone does not go through their confirmation, is their baptism incomplete?
- **If someone does not go through confirmation, do they ever receive the Holy Spirit?**
- In Acts 8:14-17 we read a description where the people of Samaria had heard and received the word of God and been baptized in the name of Jesus. The Holy Spirit doesn't come until Peter and John arrive and lay hands on the believers. In this one unique situation, the Holy Spirit didn't arrive until the apostles did. Why do you think that was so?
- Read Acts 8:18-24 to see what happens next. Could it be that in this one unique situation the Lord held back His Spirit to protect the people from the error of Simon the Magician? That the presence of the apostles was to protect the unity of the early church in explaining more fully the power of God's Spirit? How is the "intent of the heart" connected with saving faith in Jesus?
- In Acts 19:1-7 at Ephesus we read of people who had not yet received the Holy Spirit. We Apollos and those dozen men in Ephesus following the baptism of John or a saving belief in the name of Jesus? What happened when they finally believed in

Jesus (Acts 19:5-6)?

- When does someone receive the Holy Spirit according to the Bible? (1 Cor 12:13 & Eph 1:13-14)
- Is it possible to be a Christian and not have the Holy Spirit already? (Romans 8:9)
- Without confirmation are we less entitled to call God our Father?
- Without confirmation are we less united to Christ? What does Romans 8:38–39 say?
- Without confirmation do Christians have the Holy Spirit? Do they have less gifts of the Holy Spirit?
- **Are Christians incomplete without Catholic Confirmation?**
- Why would children or adults in danger of death be rushed into Confirmation?
- What does it mean to be "perfected by the Holy Spirit with the gift of Christ's fullness"?
- Where does the Bible describe God's grace as needing to be "perfected"?

IS CATHOLIC EUCHARIST NECESSARY FOR SALVATION?

Does The Wine And Bread Literally Transform To The Blood And Flesh Of Jesus?

Passages of The Catechism of the Catholic Church to Consider:

- "Our Savior instituted the Eucharistic sacrifice of his Body and Blood. This he did in order to perpetuate the sacrifice of the cross throughout the ages until he should come again" (CCC 1323)
- "The Eucharist is 'the source and summit of the Christian life.'" (CCC 1324)
- "The other sacraments, and indeed all ecclesiastical ministries and works of the apostolate, are bound up with the Eucharist and are oriented toward it." (CCC 1324)
- "in the Blessed Eucharist is contained the whole spiritual good of the Church, namely Christ himself, our Pasch." (CCC 1324) [NOTE: 'Pasch' means Passover or Easter]
- "The Eucharist is the efficacious sign and sublime cause of that communion in the divine life and that unity of the People

of God by which the Church is kept in being." (CCC 1325)

- *"Holy Sacrifice* because it makes present the one sacrifice of Christ the Savior and includes the Church's offering." (CCC 1330)
- **"Holy Communion because by this sacrifice we unite ourselves to Christ." (CCC 1331)**
- **"Holy Mass (Missa) because the liturgy in which the mystery of salvation is accomplished concludes with the sending forth (missio) of the faithful." (CCC 1332)**
- **"At the heart of the Eucharistic celebration are the bread and wine that, by the words of Christ and the invocation of the Holy Spirit, become Christ's Body and Blood." (CCC 1333)**
- "The bread and wine are brought to the altar; they will be offered by the priest in the name of Christ in the Eucharistic sacrifice in which they will become his body and blood" (CCC 1350)
- "The Church alone offers this pure oblation to the Creator" (CCC 1350)
- "no one may take part in it unless he believes that what we teach is true, has received baptism for the forgiveness of sins and new birth, and lives in keeping with what Christ taught." (CCC 1355)
- **"bread and wine which, by the power of the Holy Spirit and by the words of Christ, have become the body and blood of Christ. Christ is thus really and mysteriously made present." (CCC 1357)**
- "It is by conversion of the bread and wine into Christ's body and blood that Christ becomes present in this sacrament" (CCC 1375)
- "the making present and the sacramental offering of his unique sacrifice" (CCC 1362)
- "Because it is the memorial of Christ's Passover, the Eucharist is also a sacrifice... in the Eucharist Christ gives us the very body which he gave up for us on the cross, **the very blood which he 'poured our for man for the forgiveness of sins.'" (CCC 1365)**

- "The Eucharist is thus a sacrifice because it *re-presents* (makes present) the sacrifice of the cross, because it is its memorial and because it *applies* its fruit" (CCC 1366)
- **"its salutary power be applied to the forgiveness of sins we daily commit" (CCC 1366)**
- "Christ's sacrifice present on the altar makes it possible for all generations of Christians to be united with his offering" (CCC 1368)'
- "The Church continues to reproduce this sacrifice" (CCC 1372)
- "the whole Christ is truly, really, and substantially contained" (CCC 1374)
- "it has always been the conviction of the Church of God... that **by the consecration of the bread and wine there takes place a change of the whole substance of the bread into the substance of the body of Christ our Lord and of the whole substance of the wine into the substance of his blood. This change the holy Catholic Church has fittingly and properly called transubstantiation"** (CCC 1376)

Scriptures to Consider:

- John 6:35 "Jesus said to them, 'I am the bread of life; whoever comes to me shall not hunger, and whoever believes in me shall never thirst.'" (ESV)
- John 6:40 "For this is the will of my Father, that everyone who **looks on the Son and believes in him should have eternal life**, and I will raise him up on the last day." (ESV)
- John 6:47–51 "Truly, truly, I say to you, **whoever believes has eternal life**. [48] I am the bread of life. [49] Your fathers ate the manna in the wilderness, and they died. [50] This is the bread that comes down from heaven, so that one may eat of it and not die. [51] I am the living bread that came down from heaven. If anyone eats of this bread, he will live forever. And the bread that I will give for the life of the world is my flesh." (ESV)
- John 6:56 "Whoever feeds on my flesh and drinks my blood

abides in me, and I in him." (ESV)

- John 6:68–69 "Simon Peter answered him, "Lord, to whom shall we go? You have the words of eternal life, [69] and we have believed, and have come to know, that you are the Holy One of God." (ESV)
- John 15:4 "Abide in me, and I in you. As the branch cannot bear fruit by itself, unless it abides in the vine, neither can you, unless you abide in me." (ESV)
- 1 John 4:13 "By this we know that we abide in him and he in us, because he has given us of his Spirit." (ESV)
- 1 Corinthians 11:25–29 "In the same way also he took the cup, after supper, saying, "This cup is the new covenant in my blood. **Do this, as often as you drink it, in remembrance of me.**" [26] For as often as you **eat this bread and drink the cup**, you **proclaim the Lord's death** until he comes. [27] Whoever, therefore, **eats the bread or drinks the cup** of the Lord in an unworthy manner will be **guilty concerning the body and blood** of the Lord. [28] Let a person examine himself, then, and so **eat of the bread and drink of the cup**. [29] For anyone who eats and drinks without **discerning the body** eats and drinks judgment on himself." (ESV)
- John 19:30 "When Jesus had received the sour wine, he said, "It is finished," and he bowed his head and gave up his spirit." (ESV)
- Matthew 28:20 "I am with you always, to the end of the age." (ESV)
- 2 Corinthians 13:5 "Examine yourselves, to see whether you are in the faith. Test yourselves. Or do you not realize this about yourselves, that Jesus Christ is in you?—unless indeed you fail to meet the test!" (ESV)

Questions to Consider:

- Why does Jesus compare the manna in the desert with himself as "the bread of life" in John 6:35? What does He mean by never hunger and never thirst? Does He mean the Eucharist elements will satisfy a literal hunger and thirst? Or is He describing spiritual salvation, peace, and life through belief and trust in Jesus as the Son of God?

- **What does Jesus describe in John 6:40 & John 6:47 as bringing eternal life?**
- Why does someone literally eat and drink something? What is the purpose of food and drink? Why is trust important in the process of eating? What does the eater believe about the food?
- Does John 6:56 mean Jesus' literal flesh and blood? Why does He reference the word "abide"?
- What does John 15:4 mean by "abide"? What does that look like in a plant? What does that look like in the Christian life?
- Why does Peter tie Jesus' words to "eternal life" in John 6:68-69?
- What does it mean to be "in Christ"? What unites us to Christ? When are we united to Christ?
- What does it mean for Christ to be "in us"? When does that happen?
- **What does 1 John 4:13 say is the evidence of union with Christ?** How does this counter the Catholic concept that union with God can only happen through the Eucharist (CCC 1331)?
- Here are some more helpful Bible passages on our union with Christ: 2 Corinthians 5:17, 12:2, 13:5; John 15:4, 5, 7; 1 Corinthians 15:22; Galatians 2:20, 3:28; Ephesians 1:4, 2:10, 3:17; Philippians 3:9; 1 Thessalonians 4:16; 1 John 4:13; Colossians 1:27; Romans 8:10
- When tasting the Eucharist, does the texture or taste change with the substance? If the wine and the bread is literally transforming into the blood and flesh of Christ, then why does the texture and taste remain as wine and bread?
- Why is the Eucharist limited to the Catholic Church alone for those in good standing? Is that what the Bible teaches in 1 Corinthians 11:17-34?
- Does 1 Corinthians 11:17-34 describe the elements actually transforming in substance? Does it describe Jesus actually

being present with them during that remembrance?

- Does it describe the Church bringing judgment or the Lord bringing judgment? Does it describe individual discernment and accountability or the Church exercising oversight on who is allowed to take communion?
- **Why does 1 Corinthians 11:25–29 say eat and drink the "bread and cup" but then switch to "guilty concerning the body and blood" and then back to "bread and cup" again?**
- Is it more about "proclamation" and "remembrance" (1 Cor 11) as the purpose or an "efficacious" and "present..sacramental offering" (CCC)? Why the stark contrast in terms?
- Does the Bible say Jesus' sacrifice needs to be reproduced repeatedly? What did Jesus mean on the cross when He said "it is finished" (John 19:30)?
- What does Jesus mean when He says "I am with you always" (Matthew 28:20) and that "Jesus Christ is in you" (2 Cor 13:5)? Is that only when the Eucharist is offered? Or is He always present with believers through His Spirit?

DOES OUR EUCHARIST HELP THE DEAD?

Do We Connect To The Dead Through The Eucharist?

Passages of The Catechism of the Catholic Church to Consider:

- "In the *intercessions*, the Church indicates that the Eucharist is celebrated **in communion with** the whole Church in heaven and on earth, the living and **the dead.**" (CCC 1354)
- "To the offering of Christ are **united** not only the members still here on earth, but also **those already in the glory of heaven**. In communion with and commemorating the Blessed Virgin Mary and all the saints, the Church offers the Eucharistic sacrifice." (CCC 1370)
- "The Eucharistic sacrifice is also **offered for the faithfully departed** who 'have died in Christ but are not yet wholly purified,' **so that they may be able to enter into the light and peace of Christ**" (CCC 1371)
- "We pray for the holy fathers and bishops who have fallen asleep, and in general **for all who have fallen asleep before us**, in the belief that there is **great benefit to the souls on whose behalf the supplication is offered**" (CCC 1371)

Definitions to Consider:

Necromancy - the practice of talking to the spirits of dead people

Medium - a person through whom other persons try to communicate with the spirits of the dead

Prayer - an address (such as a petition) to God or a god in word or thought

Scriptures to Consider:

- Deuteronomy 18:10–12 "There shall not be found among you...a medium or a necromancer or one **who inquires of the dead**, for whoever does these things is an abomination to the LORD. And because of these abominations the LORD your God is driving them out before you." (ESV)
- Leviticus 19:31 "Do not turn to mediums or necromancers; do not seek them out, and so make yourselves unclean by them: I am the LORD your God." (ESV)
- Isaiah 8:19 "And when they say to you, 'Inquire of the mediums and the necromancers who chirp and mutter," **should not a people inquire of their God? Should they inquire of the dead on behalf of the living?'**" (ESV)
- 1 Samuel 28:15 "Then Samuel said to Saul, "Why have you disturbed me by bringing me up?" Saul answered, "I am in great distress, for the Philistines are warring against me, and God has turned away from me and answers me no more, either by prophets or by dreams. Therefore I have summoned you to tell me what I shall do." (ESV)
- 1 Chronicles 10:13–14 "So Saul died for his breach of faith. He broke faith with the LORD in that he did not keep the command of the LORD, and also consulted a medium, seeking guidance. [14] He did not seek guidance from the LORD. Therefore

the LORD put him to death and turned the kingdom over to David the son of Jesse." (ESV)

- Hebrews 7:27 "He has no need, like those high priests, to offer sacrifices daily, first for his own sins and then for those of the people, since he did this once for all when he offered up himself." (ESV) James 1:5 "If any of you lacks wisdom, let him ask God, who gives generously to all without reproach, and it will be given him." (ESV)
- Luke 16:30–31 "And he said, 'No, father Abraham, but if someone goes to them from the dead, they will repent.'[31] He said to him, '**If they do not hear Moses and the Prophets, neither will they be convinced if someone should rise from the dead.**'" (ESV)

Questions to Consider:

- How does one celebrate the Eucharist with the "living and the dead"? Where is that concept in the Bible?
- What does the Bible say about interactions with the dead? Sacrifices for the dead? Conversations with the dead? Is it possible? It is permitted? Is it forbidden?
- What is necromancy in the Bible? How are these descriptions of the Eucharist different or similar?
- Why does God forbid interactions with the dead? What is the danger?
- In the story of the rich man and Lazarus (Luke 16:19-31) why are the dead not allowed to communicate to the living?
- Why is the Bible ("Moses and the Prophets") described as the way for salvation to be communicated and not Penance, Eucharist, or Baptism?

IS CATHOLIC PENANCE NECESSARY FOR SALVATION?

Can Only Priests And The Catholic Church Forgive Sins?

The Sacrament of Conversion, Penance, Confession, Forgiveness, and Reconciliation (CCC 1423-24)

Passages of The Catechism of the Catholic Church to Consider:

- "The sacrament of Penance is necessary for salvation for this who have fallen after Baptism" (CCC 980)
- **"the Church possesses the power to forgive the sins of the baptized and exercises it through bishops and priests normally in the sacrament of Penance" (CCC 986)**
- "In the forgiveness of sins, both priests and sacraments are instruments through which our Lord Jesus Christ, the only author and liberal giver of salvation, wills to use in order to efface our sins and give us the grace of justification" (CCC 987)
- "reconciliation with the Church is inseparable from reconciliation with God" (CCC 1445)
- "those who, since Baptism, have fallen into grave sin and have thus lost their baptismal grace...the sacrament of Penance offers a new possibility to convert and recover the grace of jus-

tification." (CCC 1446)

- "When it arises from a love by which God is loved above all else, contrition is called 'perfect' (contrition of charity). Such contrition remits venial sins; it also obtains forgiveness of mortal sins if it includes the firm resolution to have recourse to sacramental confession as soon as possible." (CCC 1452)
- "imperfect contrition cannot obtain the forgiveness of grave sins" (CCC 1453)
- "Confession to a priest is an essential part of the sacrament of Penance" (CCC 1456)
- "the faithful is bound by an obligation faithfully to confess serious sins at least once a year" (CCC 1457)
- "without being strictly necessary, confession of everyday faults (venial sins) is nevertheless strongly recommended by the Church" (CCC 1458)
- "whoever confesses his sins...is already working with God" (CCC 1458)
- "Absolution takes away sin" (CCC 1459)
- "the sinner must still recover his full spiritual health by doing something more to make amends for the sin: he must 'make satisfaction for' or 'expiate' his sins. This satisfaction is also called 'penance'" (CCC 1459)
- "the penance the confessor imposes...must correspond as far as possible with the gravity and nature of the sins committed. It can consist of prayer, an offering, works of mercy, service of neighbor, voluntary self-denial, sacrifices...such penances help configure us to Christ...they allow us to become co-heirs with the risen Christ" (CCC 1460)
- "Indeed bishops and priests, by future of the sacrament of the Holy Orders, have the power to forgive all sins" (CCC 1461)
- "Certain particularly grave sins incur excommunication" (CCC 1463)
- "In danger of death any priest...can absolve from every sin and excommunication" (CCC 1463)
- "the whole power of the sacrament of Penance consists in restoring us to God's grace" (CCC 1468)

- "In converting to Christ through penance and faith, the sinner passes from death to life and 'does not come into judgment.' (CCC 1470)
- "those who approach the *sacrament of Penance* obtain pardon from God's mercy" (CCC 1422)
- **"It is called the *sacrament of conversion* because it makes sacramentally present Jesus' call to conversion, the first step in returning to the Father from whom one has strayed by sin." (CCC 1423)**
- **"It is called the *sacrament of Penance*, since it consecrates the Christian sinner's personal and ecclesial steps of conversion, penance, and satisfaction." (CCC 1423)**
- **"It is called the *sacrament of confession*, since the disclosure of confession of sins to a priest is an essential element of this sacrament." (CCC 1424)**
- **"It is called the *sacrament of forgiveness*, since by the priest's sacramental absolution God grants the penitent 'pardon and peace.'" (CCC 1424)**
- **"It is called the *sacrament of Reconciliation*, because it imparts to the sinner the love of God who reconciles" (CCC 1424)**
- "This is the struggle of conversion directed towards holiness and eternal life to which the Lord never ceases to call us." (CCC 1426)
- "This endeavor of conversion is not just a human work. It is the movement of a 'contrite heart,' drawn and moved by grace to respond to the merciful love of God who loved us first." (CCC 1428)
- "One who desires **to obtain reconciliation with God** and with the Church, **must confess to a priest** all the unconfessed grave sins he remembers after having carefully examined his conscience." (CCC 1493)
- "The confessor proposes the performance of certain acts of 'satisfaction' or 'penance' to be performed by the penitent in order to repair the harm caused by sin and to re-establish habits befitting a disciple of Christ." (CCC 1494)
- "**Only priests** who have received the faculty of absolving from

the authority of the Church **can forgive sins** in the name of Christ." (1495)

- "The spiritual effects of the sacrament of Penance are: - reconciliation with God by which the penitent recovers grace; - reconciliation with the Church; - remission of the eternal punishment incurred by mortal sins; - remission, at least in part, of temporal punishments from sin; - peace and serenity of conscience, and spiritual consolation; - an increase of spiritual strength for the Christian battle." (CCC 1496)

Scriptures to Consider:

- **Romans 8:39 "nor height nor depth, nor anything else in all creation, will be able to separate us from the love of God in Christ Jesus our Lord." (ESV)**
- **1 John 1:9 "If we confess our sins, he is faithful and just to forgive us our sins and to cleanse us from all unrighteousness." (ESV)**
- James 5:16 "Therefore, confess your sins to one another and pray for one another, that you may be healed. The prayer of a righteous person has great power as it is working." (ESV)
- Luke 7:48–50 "And he said to her, "Your sins are forgiven." [49] Then those who were at table with him began to say among themselves, 'Who is this, who even forgives sins?" [50] And he said to the woman, "Your faith has saved you; go in peace." (ESV)
- Romans 5:8–11 "[10] For if while we were enemies we were reconciled to God by the death of his Son, much more, now that we are reconciled, shall we be saved by his life. [11] More than that, we also rejoice in God through our Lord Jesus Christ, through whom we have now received reconciliation." (ESV)
- Romans 8:33–34 "Who shall bring any charge against God's elect? It is God who justifies. [34] Who is to condemn? Christ Jesus is the one who died—more than that, who was raised— who is at the right hand of God, who indeed is interceding for

us." (ESV)

- **Romans 8:1–2 "There is therefore now no condemnation for those who are in Christ Jesus. [2] For the law of the Spirit of life has set you free in Christ Jesus from the law of sin and death." (ESV)**
- Romans 10:1–4 "Brothers, my heart's desire and prayer to God for them is that they may be saved. [2] For I bear them witness that they have a zeal for God, but not according to knowledge. [3] For, being ignorant of the righteousness of God, and seeking to establish their own, they did not submit to God's righteousness. [4] For Christ is the end of the law for righteousness to everyone who believes." (ESV)
- Romans 10:9–10 "because, if you confess with your mouth that Jesus is Lord and believe in your heart that God raised him from the dead, you will be saved. [10] For with the heart one believes and is justified, and with the mouth one confesses and is saved." (ESV)

Questions to Consider:

- **Who has the power to forgive according to the Bible?**
- What is the purpose of confessing our sins in the Bible? Who do we go to for forgiveness? (1 John 1:9) Who do we go to for accountability, prayer, and healing? (James 5:16)
- Why do you suppose the process of confession to priest began? What are the advantages? What would be the dangers? What does the Bible say?
- After becoming a follower of Jesus, does sin separate us from the love of God?
- When did Jesus die for us? Why did He die for us? **What does Romans 8:1-2 mean?**
- How should we feel when we realize the undeserved forgiveness Jesus has shown us?
- What is the danger Paul mentions in Romans 10:1-4 about establishing their own righteousness?

- How is someone saved? How can someone know for certain they'll go to Heaven when they die?

WHAT ABOUT ABORTION & SUICIDE?

- "Formal **cooperation in an abortion constitutes a grave offense**. The Church attaches the canonical penalty of excommunication to this crime against human life." (CCC 2272)
- In Pope Francis' Apostolic Letter *Misericordia et misera* (November 20, 2016) he writes: "I henceforth grant to all priests, in virtue of their ministry, the faculty to absolve those who have committed the sin of procured abortion. The provision I had made in this regard, limited to the duration of the Extraordinary Holy Year" (http://www.vatican.va/content/francesco/en/apost_letters/documents/papa-francesco-lettera-ap_20161120_misericordia-et-misera.html)
- If the Pope has the power to forgive the sin of abortion, why does he limit it to one year for priest?
- Why does abortion typically result in excommunication? Why is the power of forgiveness restricted to Bishops on some issues like abortion?
- Why does the Catholic Church not excommunicate politicians who endorse abortion?

- "**We should not despair of the eternal salvation of persons who have taken their own lives**. By ways known to him alone, God can provide the opportunity for salutary repentance. The Church prays for this who have taken their own lives." (CCC 2283)
  - If murder is a "grave sin" and "grave sin deprives us of communion with God and therefore makes us incapable of eternal life" (CCC 1472), then how can suicide (self-murder)

result in "eternal salvation" (CCC 2283)?

- What is "salutary repentance"? Doesn't biblical repentance always involve our mind and soul? Can repentance happen after physical death? Where is that concept in the Bible?
- How is that distinct (and not contradictory) from the requirements of repentance and confession through a priest?
- Is this "exception" simply trying to tickle our "itching ears" about a tough and touchy subject?
  - 2 Timothy 4:3 "For the time is coming when people will not endure sound teaching, but having itching ears they will accumulate for themselves teachers to suit their own passions" (ESV)
- Where does the Bible talk about praying for the dead?
- SEE: "What Does the Bible Say about Abortion?" www.trustworthyword.com/what-does-the-bible-say-about-abortion
- SEE: "What Does the Bible Say about Suicide?" www.trustworthyword.com/suicide

IS PETER THE FIRST POPE (BISHOP OF ROME)?

Passages of The Catechism of the Catholic Church to Consider:

- "Simon Peter holds first place in the college of the Twelve"(CCC 551)
- "Peter has confessed: 'You are the Christ, the Son of the living God.' Our Lord then declared to him: 'You are Peter, and on this rock I will build my Church, and the gates of Hades will not prevail against it.'" (CCC 552)
- "Christ, the 'living stone,' thus assures his Church, built on Peter, of victory over the power of death. Because of the faith he confessed Peter will remain the unshakeable rock of the Church. His mission will be to keep this faith from every lapse and to strengthen his brothers in it." (CCC 552)
- "Jesus entrusted a specific authority to Peter: 'I will give you the keys of the kingdom of heaven, and whatever you bind on earth shall be bound in heaven and whatever you loose on earth shall be loosed in heaven.' The 'power of the keys' designates **authority to govern the house of God, which is the Church**." (CCC 553)
- **"The power to 'bind and loose' connotes the authority to absolve sins, to pronounce doctrinal judgments, and to make disciplinary judgments in the Church."** (CCC 553)

- "Jesus entrusted this authority to the Church through the ministry of the apostles and in particular through the ministry of Peter, the only one to whom he specifically **entrusted the keys of the kingdom**" (CCC 553)

Scriptures to Consider:

- Luke 6:47–48 "Everyone who **comes to me** and **hears my words** and **does them**, I will show you what he is like: he is like a man building a house, who dug deep and laid the **foundation on the rock**. And when a flood arose, the stream broke against that house and could not shake it, because it had been well built." (ESV)
- Mark 8:27–30 "And Jesus went on with his disciples to the villages of Caesarea Philippi. And on the way he asked his disciples, "Who do people say that I am?" [28] And they told him, "John the Baptist; and others say, Elijah; and others, one of the prophets." [29] And he asked them, "But who do you say that I am?" Peter answered him, **"You are the Christ."** [30] And he strictly charged them to tell no one about him." (ESV)
- Luke 9:20 "Then he said to them, "But who do you say that I am?" And Peter answered, **"The Christ of God**." (ESV)
- Luke 9:32 "Now Peter and those who were with him were heavy with sleep, but when they became fully awake they saw his glory and the two men who stood with him." (ESV)
- John 13:8–10 "Peter said to him, "You shall never wash my feet." Jesus answered him, "If I do not wash you, you have no share with me." [9] Simon Peter said to him, "Lord, not my feet only but also my hands and my head!" [10] Jesus said to him, "The one who has bathed does not need to wash, except for his feet, but is completely clean. And you are clean, but not every one of you." (ESV)
- Matthew 14:30–31 "But when he saw the wind, he was afraid, and beginning to sink he cried out, 'Lord, save me.' [31] Jesus immediately reached out his hand and took hold of him, saying

to him, 'O you of little faith, why did you doubt?'" (ESV)

- Matthew 16:22–23 "And Peter took him aside and began to rebuke him, saying, "Far be it from you, Lord! This shall never happen to you." [23] But he turned and said to Peter, "Get behind me, Satan! You are a hindrance to me. For you are not setting your mind on the things of God, but on the things of man." (ESV)

- Matthew 17:4–5 "And Peter said to Jesus, 'Lord, it is good that we are here. If you wish, I will make three tents here, one for you and one for Moses and one for Elijah.' [5] He was still speaking when, behold, a bright cloud overshadowed them, and a voice from the cloud said, "This is my beloved Son, with whom I am well pleased; listen to him." (ESV)

- Matthew 26:33–35 "Peter answered him, "Though they all fall away because of you, I will never fall away." [34] Jesus said to him, "Truly, I tell you, this very night, before the rooster crows, you will deny me three times." [35] Peter said to him, "Even if I must die with you, I will not deny you!" And all the disciples said the same." (ESV)

- Matthew 26:40–43 "And he came to the disciples and found them sleeping. And he said to Peter, "So, could you not watch with me one hour? [41] Watch and pray that you may not enter into temptation. The spirit indeed is willing, but the flesh is weak." [42] Again, for the second time, he went away and prayed, "My Father, if this cannot pass unless I drink it, your will be done." [43] And again he came and found them sleeping, for their eyes were heavy." (ESV)

- John 18:10–11 "Then Simon Peter, having a sword, drew it and struck the high priest's servant and cut off his right ear. (The servant's name was Malchus.) [11] So Jesus said to Peter, "Put your sword into its sheath; shall I not drink the cup that the Father has given me?" (ESV)

- Matthew 26:56 "But all this has taken place that the Scriptures of the prophets might be fulfilled." Then all the disciples left him and fled." (ESV)

- Matthew 26:69–75 "Now Peter was sitting outside in the

courtyard. And a servant girl came up to him and said, "You also were with Jesus the Galilean." [70] But he denied it before them all, saying, "I do not know what you mean." [71] And when he went out to the entrance, another servant girl saw him, and she said to the bystanders, "This man was with Jesus of Nazareth." [72] And again he denied it with an oath: "I do not know the man." [73] After a little while the bystanders came up and said to Peter, "Certainly you too are one of them, for your accent betrays you." [74] Then he began to invoke a curse on himself and to swear, "I do not know the man." And immediately the rooster crowed. [75] And Peter remembered the saying of Jesus, "Before the rooster crows, you will deny me three times." And he went out and wept bitterly." (ESV)

- Luke 22:61 "And the Lord turned and looked at Peter. And Peter remembered the saying of the Lord, how he had said to him, "Before the rooster crows today, you will deny me three times." (ESV)
- John 21:21 "When Peter saw him, he said to Jesus, 'Lord, what about this man?'"
- Acts 10:13–16 "And there came a voice to him: "Rise, Peter; kill and eat." [14] But Peter said, **"By no means, Lord**; for I have never eaten anything that is common or unclean." [15] And the voice came to him again a second time, "What God has made clean, do not call common." [16] This happened three times, and the thing was taken up at once to heaven." (ESV)
- Galatians 2:11–14 "But when Cephas came to Antioch, I opposed him to his face, because he stood condemned. [12] For before certain men came from James, he was eating with the Gentiles; but when they came he drew back and separated himself, fearing the circumcision party. [13] And the rest of the Jews **acted hypocritically** along with him, so that even Barnabas was led astray by their hypocrisy. [14] But when I saw that their conduct was **not in step with the truth of the gospel**, I said to Cephas before them all, 'If you, though a Jew, live like a Gentile and not like a Jew, how can you force the Gentiles to live like Jews?'" (ESV)

Questions to Consider:

- Why does Jesus, right after this affirmation to Peter, then rebuke Peter and say **"Get behind me, Satan!** You are a hindrance to me. For you are not setting your mind on the things of God, but on the things of man."? (Matthew 16:21-23 ESV). Is this a characteristic of Papal Infallibility?
- In parallel accounts of Matthew 16:13-20 **(Mark 8:27-30 & Luke 9:20)**, why does Jesus **not mention the claim of Peter being the rock of the church and having the keys to "bind and loose"**? If it is that important to the Church why is it only mentioned one book of the Bible?
- What are keys used for? What "unlocks" the doors of the Kingdom of Heaven? What does Jesus say in John 3:3? What does Paul say it takes to be saved in Romans 10:9-10? John in Revelation 3:20?
  - John 3:3 "Jesus answered him, 'Truly, truly, I say to you, unless one is born again he cannot see the kingdom of God.'" (ESV)
  - Romans 10:9–10 "because, if you confess with your mouth that Jesus is Lord and believe in your heart that God raised him from the dead, you will be saved. [10] For with the heart one believes and is justified, and with the mouth one confesses and is saved." (ESV)
  - Revelation 3:20 "Behold, I stand at the door and knock. If anyone hears my voice and opens the door, I will come in to him and eat with him, and he with me." (ESV)
- What does Jesus' warning in Matthew 23:13 mean in terms of doors and the kingdom of heaven?
  - Matt23:13 "But woe to you, scribes and Pharisees, hypocrites! For you shut the kingdom of heaven in people's faces. For you neither enter yourselves nor allow those who would enter to go in."
- What about "bind" and "loose" being used in **Matthew**

18:15-20 in terms of church discipline? Why is Peter's authority not mentioned in this passage? Why is this authority extended to the church body?

- **What about when Peter was wrong**...correcting Jesus (John 13:8-10), doubting Jesus with little faith (Matthew 14:30-31), rebuking Jesus (Matthew 16:22-23), misunderstanding the Transfiguration (Matthew 17:1-8), questioning Jesus, promising to never abandon Jesus (Matthew 26:33-35), falling asleep on the Mount of Transfiguration and the Garden of Gethsemane (Luke 9:32 and Matthew 26:40–43), impulsive (John 18:10–11), abandoning Jesus (Matthew 26:56), denying Jesus (Matthew 26:69–75) to in His presence (Luke 22:61), blame shifting (John 21:21), refusing to obey God's voice in a vision (Acts 10:13-16), and being hypocritically legalistic and exclusive ("not in step with the truth of the Gospel" Galatians 2:11-14). **How do we process that with claims of Papal infallibility? Why did Paul correct him if Peter is the first pope?**
- Did Peter ever go to Rome? Why, historically speaking, does the Catholic Church become associated with Rome? Was the **Edict of Milan in 313 A.D.** by Constantine helpful or harmful to Christianity? Did the Roman influence and control co-opt the Catholic Church for its own use? Was the biblical fidelity compromised in order to adapt the biblical message to be syncretized (changed) into a more palatable flavor for a variety of cultural contexts (i.e. by adding purgatory, indulgences, icons, prayers to the dead, etc.)?
- **So is Jesus saying that the church is being built on the person of Peter, or the proclamation of the Gospel, that Jesus is the Christ, the Son of the living God?**
- Considering Luke 6:47-48; What is the foundation and rock Jesus is referencing?
- In the Bible, is the test of faithfulness one of succession and lineage or one of consistency with God's words?
- Matthew 16:17 "And Jesus answered him, 'Blessed are you, Simon Bar-Jonah! For flesh and blood has not revealed this to you, but my Father who is in heaven.'" (ESV)

- Is Jesus conferring a blessing or acknowledging the blessing of God?
- Matthew 16:18 "And I tell you, you are Peter, and on this rock I will build my church, and the gates of hell shall not prevail against it." (ESV)
  - Is this verse more about Peter and his lineage of popes, or about looking upon and believing in Jesus? What do we do with the many passages about Jesus who conquers death/Hades/Hell (Romans 8:2; Acts 2:24) because "death no longer is master over Him" (Romans 6:9), thus bringing his church (gathered ones) together as "conquerors" (Romans 8:37-39).
- When 1 Timothy 3:1-7 and Titus 1:5-9 lay out the office of elder/overseer/bishop/pastor why is there no distinction made about a Pope or head Bishop? Why is there always a plurality of elders referenced in the leadership of local churches?
- Ephesians 2:19–22 "So then you are no longer strangers and aliens, but you are fellow citizens with the saints and members of the household of God, [20] built on the foundation of the apostles and prophets, Christ Jesus himself being the cornerstone, [21] in whom the whole structure, being joined together, grows into a holy temple in the Lord. [22] In him you also are being built together into a dwelling place for God by the Spirit." (ESV)
  - In this description of the church, why is Peter not referenced? Why is there no reference to the oversight of a head/lead/arch Bishop or Pope? Is the sole reference to Jesus a reference back to the foundation/rock of the church being on Jesus alone and not on human authority?
- To whom was the name "rock" assigned in the Old Testament (Deut. 32:4, 15, 18, 30–31)? To whom does 1 Corinthians 10:4 assign the name rock?
  - Deuteronomy 32:4 "The Rock, his work is perfect, for all his ways are justice. A God of faithfulness and without iniquity, just and upright is he." (ESV)
  - 1 Corinthians 10:4 "all drank the same spiritual drink. For they drank from the spiritual Rock that followed them, and

the Rock was Christ." (ESV)

- Acts 8:14 "Now when the apostles at Jerusalem heard that Samaria had received the word of God, they sent to them Peter and John" (ESV)
  - If Peter is authoritatively in charge of the church, why is he "sent" by the other apostles?
- If Peter has the authority to forgive sins (per CCC 982, 986, 987), where does he do that in the Bible? Like the ways in which Jesus expresses His authority to forgive sins (Matthew 9:6, Mark 2:10, Luke 5:24; 7:49, Acts 10:43, Colossians 1:14, 1 John 1:9)?
  - "There is no offense, however serious, that the Church cannot forgive" (CCC 982)
  - "the Church possesses the power to forgive the sins of the baptized and exercises it through bishops and priests normally in the sacrament of Penance" (CCC 986)
  - "In the forgiveness of sins, both priests and sacraments are instruments through which our Lord Jesus Christ, the only author and liberal giver of salvation, wills to use in order to efface our sins and give us the grace of justification" (CCC 987)
- John 20:21–23 "Jesus said to them again, "Peace be with you. As the Father has sent me, even so I am sending you." [22] And when he had said this, he breathed on them and said to them, "Receive the Holy Spirit. [23] If you forgive the sins of any, they are forgiven them; if you withhold forgiveness from any, it is withheld." (ESV)
  - What did Jesus just show them in John 20:20? Why was this evidence important to their mission? How do the disciples' response demonstrate their belief?
  - What is the message they are being sent with? How is the Holy Spirit connected to Jesus' sending of his disciples?
  - Since the words for "forgive" are written as perfect-tense verbs, they represent actions completed in the past with continuing effects into the present and future. Doesn't this appear to point more towards Christian responsibility to proclaim the Gospel message of forgiveness of sins in the power

of the Holy Spirit?

- ESV Study Bible NOTE: "The idea is not that individual Christians or churches have authority on their own to forgive or not forgive people, but rather that as the church proclaims the gospel message of forgiveness of sins in the power of the Holy Spirit (see v. 22), it proclaims that those who believe in Jesus have their sins forgiven, and that those who do not believe in him do not have their sins forgiven—which simply reflects what God in heaven has already done (cf. note on Matt. 16:19)."
- Are Christians called to be judges withholding forgiveness from one another? Or are they called to be ambassadors or messengers of the message of forgiveness found in the Gospel?
  - 2 Corinthians 5:20 "Therefore, we are ambassadors for Christ, God making his appeal through us. We implore you on behalf of Christ, be reconciled to God." (ESV)

DID PETER HAVE AUTHORITY OVER ALL THE APOSTLES?

Passages of The Catechism of the Catholic Church to Consider:

- **"The sole Church of Christ [is that] which our Savior, after his Resurrection, entrusted to Peter's pastoral care**, commissioning him and the other apostles to extend and rule it. ... This Church, constituted and organized as a society in the present world, subsists in (*subsistit in*) the Catholic Church, which is **governed by the successor of Peter and by the bishops in communion with him." (CCC 816)**

- "For it is through Christ's Catholic Church alone, which is the universal hope toward salvation, that the fullness of the means of salvation can be obtained" (CCC 816)

- "Just as **the office which the Lord confided to Peter alone**, as first of the apostles, **destined to be transmitted to his successors, is a permanent one, so also endures the office**...Hence the Church teaches that 'the bishops have by divine institution taken the place of the apostles as pastors of the Church, in such wise that **whoever listens to them is listening to Christ and whoever despises them despises Christ and him who sent Christ**" (CCC 862)

Scriptures to Consider:

- Mark 3:14–19 "And he appointed twelve (whom he also named apostles) so that they might be with him and he might send them out to preach [15] and have authority to cast out demons. [16] He appointed the twelve: Simon (to whom he gave the name Peter); [17] James the son of Zebedee and John the brother of James (to whom he gave the name Boanerges, that is, Sons of Thunder); [18] Andrew, and Philip, and Bartholomew, and Matthew, and Thomas, and James the son of Alphaeus, and Thaddaeus, and Simon the Zealot, [19] and Judas Iscariot, who betrayed him." (ESV)
- Acts 11:4 "But Peter began and explained it to them in order" (ESV)
- Matthew 15:15 "But Peter said to him, 'Explain the parable to us.'" (ESV)
- Acts 2:14 "But Peter, standing with the eleven, lifted up his voice and addressed them: 'Men of Judea and all who dwell in Jerusalem, let this be known to you, and give ear to my words.'" (ESV)
- Acts 2:38 "And Peter said to them, "Repent and be baptized every one of you in the name of Jesus Christ for the forgiveness of your sins, and you will receive the gift of the Holy Spirit." (ESV)
- Acts 2:42 "And they devoted themselves **to the apostles' teaching** and the fellowship, to the breaking of bread and the prayers." (ESV)
- Acts 5:29 "But Peter and the apostles answered, **'We must obey God rather than men.'"** (ESV).
- Matthew 18:17–20 "If he refuses to listen to them, tell it to the church. And if he refuses to listen even to the church, let him be to you as a Gentile and a tax collector. [18] Truly, I say to you, whatever you bind on earth shall be bound in heaven, and whatever you loose on earth shall be loosed in heaven. [19] Again I say to you, if two of you agree on earth about anything

they ask, it will be done for them by my Father in heaven. [20] For where two or three are gathered in my name, there am I among them." (ESV)

- 1 Corinthians 16:10 "When Timothy comes, see that you put him at ease among you, for he is doing the work of the Lord, as I am."
- 1 Corinthians 16:16 **"be subject to such as these, and to every fellow worker and laborer."**
- 2 Corinthians 8:23 "As for Titus, he is my partner and fellow worker for your benefit. And as for our brothers, they are messengers of the churches, the glory of Christ."
- Revelation 21:14 "And the wall of the city had twelve foundations, and **on them were the twelve names of the twelve apostles of the Lamb."** (ESV)
- Acts 10:44–48 "While Peter was still saying these things, the Holy Spirit fell on all who heard the word. [45] And the believers from among the circumcised who had come with Peter were amazed, because the gift of the Holy Spirit was poured out even on the Gentiles. [46] For they were hearing them speaking in tongues and extolling God. Then Peter declared, [47] "Can anyone withhold water for baptizing these people, who have received the Holy Spirit just as we have?" [48] And he commanded them to be baptized in the name of Jesus Christ. Then they asked him to remain for some days." (ESV)
- Romans 1:7 "To all those in Rome who are loved by God and **called to be saints"**

Questions to Consider:

- The Catechism of the Catholic Church references Jesus" 'choice of the Twelve with Peter as their head" (CCC 765) and solely references Mark 3:14-15 for the evidence of this claim. **Does Mark 3:14-15 reference Peter as the head of the church in any Bible? Why not?**
- Why do these big claims (CCC 816 & CCC 862) have no Scrip-

ture cited for their support in *The Catechism of the Catholic Church*?

- Why does Peter have to answer to the authority of the church at Jerusalem in Acts 11 if he is the head authority?
- Did Peter act more like the spokesman for the apostles or as the authoritative leader of the apostles?
- Why does Paul appear and teach so much more than Peter in the New Testament if Peter was the first Pope? What about the other leaders who feature prominently in the early church like John and James (brothers of Jesus)?
- Why are some decisions made by the church body and not solely by Peter?
- Why did believers receive the Holy Spirit before taking the Eucharist in Acts 2:38? Isn't that out of order for the Catholic sacraments?
- **Why would Peter speak Acts 5:29 if he was also asserting Papal infallibility and the Magesterium of the Church?**
- Why does church discipline's final step in Matthew 18:17-20 speak about coming before the gathered body of the church and not the church leadership/pastors/priests/bishops? Why is this binding and loosing language used in reference to the church body ("two or three are gathered in my name") and not in reference to Peter or a Pope/Bishop/Priest?
- Isn't the "loosing and binding" authority shared with the local churches? In 1 Corinthians 5:1-13, 2 Corinthians 13:10, Titus 2:15, and Titus 3:10-11
- Is the authority of Timothy and Titus based on them being a bishop and having apostolic authority, or being a "fellow laborer"?
- **If the future heavenly holy city of Jerusalem has the name of the apostles on it (Revelation 21:14), why doesn't it recognize Peter as the head, or the first Pope/Bishop, or with some other sort of special recognition?**
- Why are all alive Christians referred to as saints in the New Testament? Is this term only referring to deceased believers specially designated by the Catholic Church?

DID PETER CALL HIMSELF A POPE OR BISHOP?

Scriptures to Consider:

- 1 Peter 1:1 "Peter, an apostle of Jesus Christ"
- 2 Peter 1:1 "Simeon Peter, a servant and apostle of Jesus Christ"
- 1 Peter 2:25 "For you were straying like sheep, but have now returned to the Shepherd and Overseer of your souls"
- 1 Corinthians 1:12–17 "**What I mean is that each one of you says, "I follow Paul," or "I follow Apollos," or "I follow Cephas," or "I follow Christ." [13] Is Christ divided?** Was Paul crucified for you? Or were you baptized in the name of Paul? [14] I thank God that I baptized none of you except Crispus and Gaius, [15] so that no one may say that you were baptized in my name. [16] (I did baptize also the household of Stephanas. Beyond that, I do not know whether I baptized anyone else.) [17] For Christ did not send me to baptize but to preach the gospel, and not with words of eloquent wisdom, lest the cross of Christ be emptied of its power." (ESV)
- 1 Corinthians 3:4–9 "For when one says, "I follow Paul," and another, "I follow Apollos," are you not being merely human?" [5] What then is Apollos? What is Paul? Servants through whom you believed, as the Lord assigned to each. [6] I planted, Apollos watered, but God gave the growth. [7] So neither he who plants nor he who waters is anything, but

89

only God who gives the growth. [8] He who plants and he who waters are one, and each will receive his wages according to his labor. [9] For we are God's fellow workers. You are God's field, God's building." (ESV)

- 1 Corinthians 3:19–23 "For the wisdom of this world is folly with God. For it is written, "He catches the wise in their craftiness," [20] and again, "The Lord knows the thoughts of the wise, that they are futile." [21] **So let no one boast in men.** For all things are yours, [22] **whether Paul or Apollos or Cephas** or the world or life or death or the present or the future—all are yours, [23] and **you are Christ's, and Christ is God's.**" (ESV)
- 1 Peter 5:1–2 "So I exhort the elders among you, as a fellow elder and a witness of the sufferings of Christ, as well as a partaker in the glory that is going to be revealed: [2] shepherd the flock of God that is among you, exercising oversight, **not under compulsion, but willingly,** as God would have you; not for shameful gain, but eagerly" (ESV)

Questions to Consider:

- **Why doesn't Peter refer to himself more than just a servant or apostle?** If he was leading the church authoritatively wouldn't he have asserted so in his introduction?
- Is there anywhere in the Bible where Peter asserts his authority, role, or power over the other apostles?
- Specifically as the foundation of the church, the pope, why doesn't Peter mention apostolic succession anywhere in the Bible?
- Why are there so many repeated warnings in 1 Corinthians 1 & 3 about following people by name? If Peter wanted the church to follow his leadership and name, why doesn't he say so in his writings (1 & 2 Peter)?
- Why does Peter always point to Jesus instead of the church and its sacraments as the hope of salvation? Why does 1 and 2 Peter (the writings of Peter) sound so different from *The Catechism of the Catholic Church*?

- **Why does the Catholic Church assert the obligation or compulsion for obedience versus the description of 1 Peter 5:1-2 saying "not under compulsion, but willingly"?**

WAS PETER MARRIED? IS PRIESTLY CELIBACY BIBLICAL?

Passages of The Catechism of the Catholic Church to Consider:

- "All the ordained ministers of the Latin Church, with the exception of permanent deacons are normally **chosen from among men of faith who live a celibate life and who intend to remain celibate 'for the sake of the kingdom of heaven.'**" (CCC 1579)
- "In the Eastern Churches a different discipline has been in force for many centuries…married men can be ordained as deacons and priests. This practice has long been considered legitimate" (CCC 1580)
- **"Celibacy is a sign of this new life of the service of which the Church's minister is consecrated**; accepted with a joyous heart celibacy radiantly proclaims the Reign of God." (CCC 1579)

Scriptures to Consider:

- Matthew 19:12 "For there are eunuchs who have been so from birth, and there are eunuchs who have been made eunuchs by men, and there are eunuchs who have made themselves eunuchs for the sake of the kingdom of heaven. Let the one who is able to receive this receive it." (ESV)

- Matthew 8:14 "And when Jesus entered Peter's house, he saw his mother-in-law lying sick with a fever." (ESV)
- Mark 1:30 "Now Simon's mother-in-law lay ill with a fever, and immediately they told him about her." (ESV)
- Luke 4:38 "And he arose and left the synagogue and entered Simon's house. Now Simon's mother-in-law was ill with a high fever, and they appealed to him on her behalf. (ESV)
- **1 Corinthians 9:5 "Do we not have the right to take along a believing wife, as do the other apostles and the brothers of the Lord and Cephas?" (ESV)**
- 1 Timothy 3:2 "Therefore an overseer must be above reproach, the husband of one wife, sober-minded, self-controlled, respectable, hospitable, able to teach" (ESV)
- Titus 1:6 "if anyone is above reproach, the husband of one wife, and his children are believers and not open to the charge of debauchery or insubordination." (ESV)
- 1 Timothy 4:3 "**who forbid marriage** and require abstinence from foods that God created to be received with thanksgiving by those who believe and know the truth." (ESV)

Questions to Consider:

- Does Matthew 19:12 sound like a voluntary choice among believers or a mandate for all priests?
- Is celibacy is a "sign of this new life of service", then why wasn't Peter single?
- Why does the encouragement of 1 Corinthians 9:5 encourage marriage in the example of Peter and Jesus' brothers?
- In the Biblical descriptions of qualifications (1 Timothy 3:1-7 and Titus 1:5-9) for overseers, bishops, elder, or pastors, are there ever any encouragements or mandates for singleness? Why do these passages both reference the church leaders as being married?
- If the Catholic Church is reconsidering its position on this issue, was it wrong in the past? What other issues may they

have not spoken from the unchanging revelation of God?
- Does the warning of 1 Timothy 4:3 apply to the Catholic Church? For priestly celibacy? For lenten fasting?

WHAT IS VENERATION? IS MARY OUR MOTHER?

Should Mary Be Venerated?

Our word usage matters…what do we mean by the words we use? Are they accurate descriptions of our actions?

> NOTE: The same word "venerate" is used to describe the Bible, images, Mary, saints, & angels.

Merriam-Webster's Definitions:

Veneration - "respect or awe inspired by the dignity, wisdom, dedication, or talent of a person"

Worship - "excessive admiration of or devotion to a person"

Adoration - "strong feelings of love or admiration"

Sacred - "worthy of religious veneration, holy, dedicated or set apart for the service or worship of a deity"

Prayer - "an address (such as a petition) to God or a god in word or thought"

Genuflect - "to touch the knee to the floor or ground especially in worship"

Passages of The Catechism of the Catholic Church to Consider:

- "the Church venerates in Mary the purest realization of faith" (CCC 149)
- "the Church has always venerated the Scriptures as she venerates the Lord's Body" (CCC 103)
- "Through the icon of Christ and his works of salvation, it is he whom we adore." (CCC 1192)
- "Through sacred images of of the holy Mother of God, of the angels and the saints, we venerate the persons represented" (CCC 1192)
- "Jesus is Mary's only son, but her spiritual motherhood extends to all men" (CCC 501)

Scriptures to Consider:

- Matthew 11:11 "Truly, I say to you, among those born of women there has arisen no one greater than John the Baptist. Yet the one who is least in the kingdom of heaven is greater than he." (ESV)
- Ps 18:3 "I call upon the LORD, who is worthy to be praised, & I am saved from my enemies." (ESV)
- Psalm 71:16 "With the mighty deeds of the Lord GOD I will come; I will remind them of your righteousness, yours alone." (ESV)
- Psalm 72:18 "Blessed be the LORD, the God of Israel, who alone does wondrous things." (ESV)
- Isaiah 26:13 "O LORD our God...your name alone we bring to remembrance." (ESV)
- Philippians 4:8 "Finally, brothers, whatever is true, whatever is honorable, whatever is just, whatever is pure, whatever is lovely, whatever is commendable, if there is any excellence, if there is anything worthy of praise, think about these things." (ESV)

Questions to Consider:
- **According the dictionary definitions, how different are the**

words "veneration", "worship", "adoration", and "sacred"?

- Where is the line crossed from "veneration" to "worship" or "adoration"?
- What are the differences and similarities in Catholic practices of veneration to Mary and worship to God? What protections are in place so people do not have more affection for Mary than Jesus?
- Considering what Jesus said about John the Baptist in Matthew 11:11, why is he not given more honor than Mary in the Bible? **Why is Mary not referenced as "our Mother" in the Bible?**
- Does Psalm 71:16, 72:8 or Isaiah 26:13 focus on angels or saints? Why not
- Does the Bible use the word "veneration"? What does Philippians 4:8 say to do about things that are "worthy of praise"? Do Catholic practices go beyond "thinking about these things"?
- **Does the Bible command the use of images, prayers, the Eucharist, or sacrifices in order to give honor to Mary, the saints, or angels?**

WAS MARY ALWAYS SAVED? DID MARY NEVER SIN?

Passages of The Catechism of the Catholic Church to Consider:

- "Through the centuries the Church has become ever more aware that Mary, "full of grace", was **redeemed from the moment of her conception**. That is what the dogma of the Immaculate Conception confesses, as Pope Pius IX proclaimed in 1854: 'The Most Blessed Virgin Mary was, from the first moment of her conception, by a singular grace and privilege of almighty God and by virtue of the merits of Jesus Christ, Savior of the human race, **preserved immune from all stain of original sin.**" (CCC 491)
- "**Mary remained free of every personal sin her whole life long**" (CCC 493)
- "from the first instant of her conception, she was totally preserved from the stain of original sin and she remained pure from all personal sin throughout her life" (CCC 508)
- "the Immaculate Virgin, preserved free from all stain of original sin" (CCC 966)
- "her **complete adherence to the Father's will**" (CCC 967)

Scriptures to Consider:

- **1 John 1:8 "If we say we have no sin, we deceive ourselves, and the truth is not in us." (ESV)**
- **Romans 3:23 "for all have sinned and fall short of the glory of God" (ESV)**
- Romans 3:10 "None is righteous, no, not one" (ESV)
- Romans 5:12 "Therefore, just as sin came into the world through one man, and death through sin, and so death spread to all men because all sinned"
- Romans 5:18–19 "Therefore, as one trespass led to condemnation for all men, so one act of righteousness leads to justification and life for all men. [19] For as by the one man's disobedience the many were made sinners, so by the one man's obedience the many will be made righteous." (ESV)
- Psalm 51:5 "Behold, I was brought forth in iniquity, and in sin did my mother conceive me."
- Jeremiah 17: 9 "The heart is deceitful above all things, and desperately sick; who can understand it?"
- 2 Corinthians 5:21 "**For our sake he made him to be sin who knew no sin,** so that in him we might become the righteousness of God." (ESV)

Questions to Consider:

- Did Jesus or any of the apostles mention that Mary was sinless?
- Does any part of the Bible mention someone (apart from Jesus) who was sinless?
- Is not the claim to Mary's sinlessness putting her on the same level as Jesus?
- If the implication is that Mary had to be sinless for Jesus to be unstained by sin, then wouldn't that logic extend to Mary's parents as well? When would that line of "sinlessness" end?
- What does 1 John 1:8 say about claiming to not have sin?

What does that imply about *The Catechism of the Catholic Church?*"

IS MARY THE CAUSE OF SALVATION?

Passages of The Catechism of the Catholic Church to Consider:

- **"Being obedient she became the cause of salvation for herself and for the whole human race." (CCC 494)**
- "Hence not a few of the early Fathers gladly assert ... : 'The knot of Eve's disobedience was untied by Mary's obedience: what the Virgin Eve bound through her disbelief, Mary loosened by her faith.' Comparing her with Eve, they call Mary 'the Mother of all living' and frequently claim: **'Death through Eve, life through Mary." (CCC 494)**
- "The Virgin Mary **'cooperated through free faith and obedience in human salvation**. ... By her obedience she became the new Eve, mother of the living." (CCC 511)
- **"by your prayers, will deliver our souls from death" (CCC 966)**
- "restoring supernatural life to souls" (CCC 968)
- **"the Blessed Virgin...under the titles of Advocate, Helper, Benefactress, and Mediatrix" (CCC 969)**
- "collaborating with the whole work her Son was to accomplish" (CCC 973)
- "the new Eve, the Mother of the Church, continues in heaven to exercise her maternal role on behalf of the members of Christ" (CCC 975)
- "she is inseparably linked with the saving work of her Son" (CCC 1172)

- "The Gospel reveals to us how Mary prays and intercedes in faith. At Cana, the mother of Jesus asks her son for the needs of a wedding feast; this is the sign of another feast - that of the wedding of the Lamb where he gives his body and blood at the request of the Church, his Bride. It is at the hour of the New Covenant, at the foot of the cross, that Mary is heard as the Woman, the new Eve, the true 'Mother of all the living.'" (CCC 2618)
- "by asking Mary to pray for us....we address ourselves to the **'Mother of Mercy,' the All-Holy One**. We give ourselves our to her now...our trust broadens further...to surrender 'the hour of our death' wholly to her care. ... May she welcome us as our mother at the hour of our passing to lead us to her son, Jesus, in paradise" (CCC 2677)

Scriptures to Consider:

- NOTE: The Bible never mentions Mary being "full of grace" (but uses that phrase with Jesus and Stephen), re-deemed from conception, or sinless. While the Bible describes Mary as "highly favored" (Luke 1:28) and "blessed . . . among women" (Luke 1:42) it does not support the claim to sinless-ness.
- Romans 3:23–24 "for all have sinned and fall short of the glory of God, [24] and are justified by his grace as a gift, through the redemption that is in Christ Jesus" (ESV)
- Romans 5:12 "Therefore, just as sin came into the world through one man, and death through sin, and so death spread to all men because all sinned" (ESV)
- 1 John 1:8-10 "If we say we have no sin, we deceive ourselves, and the truth is not in us. 9 If we confess our sins, he is faithful and just to forgive us our sins and to cleanse us from all un-righteousness. 10 If we say we have not sinned, we make him a liar, and his word is not in us"
- John 2:4 "Jesus said to her, **'Woman, what does this have to do**

with me?'"

- Acts 6:8 "Stephen, full of grace and power, was doing great wonders and signs among the people."
- John 1:14 "the Word became flesh and dwelt among us, and we have seen his glory, glory as of the only Son from the Father, full of grace and truth"
- Psalm 51:5 "Behold, I was brought forth in iniquity, and in sin did my mother conceive me."
- Romans 5:17 "For if, because of one man's trespass, death reigned through that one man, much more will those who receive the abundance of grace and the free gift of righteousness reign in life through the one man Jesus Christ." (ESV)
- Romans 5:10 "For if while we were enemies we were reconciled to God by the death of his Son, much more, now that we are reconciled, shall we be saved by his life." (ESV)
- John 10:28 "I give them eternal life, and they will never perish"
- 1 John 2:1 "My little children, I am writing these things to you so that you may not sin. But if anyone does sin, we have **an advocate with the Father, Jesus Christ the righteous**." (ESV) Romans 5:18 "Therefore, as one trespass led to condemnation for all men, so one act of righteousness leads to justification and life for all men." (ESV)
- 1 Corinthians 15:45 "Thus it is written, "The first man Adam became a living being"; the last Adam became a life-giving spirit." (ESV)
- John 14:16 "I will ask the Father, and he will give you another Helper, to be with you forever" (ESV)
- Hebrews 13:6 "So we can confidently say, 'The Lord is my helper; I will not fear; what can man do to me?'" (ESV)
- John 14:26 "But **the Helper, the Holy Spirit**, whom the Father will send in my name, he will teach you all things and bring to your remembrance all that I have said to you." (ESV)
- John 15:26 "But when the Helper comes, whom I will send to you from the Father, the Spirit of truth, who proceeds from the Father, he will bear witness about me." (ESV)

- John 16:7 "Nevertheless, I tell you the truth: it is to your advantage that I go away, for if I do not go away, the Helper will not come to you. But if I go, I will send him to you." (ESV)
- 1 Timothy 2:5 "For there is one God, and there is **one mediator** between God and men, the man Christ Jesus" (ESV)
- John 2:4 "And Jesus said to her, 'Woman, what does this have to do with me? My hour has not yet come.'" (ESV)
- 1 Peter 4:19 "Therefore let those who suffer according to God's will **entrust their souls to a faithful Creator** while doing good." (ESV)

Questions to Consider:

- **Why is Mary given titles that are only biblically used as titles to describe God Himself? "Advocate, Helper, Benefactress, and Mediatrix [Mediator]" Why are there no biblical passages giving Mary these titles?**
- Did Jesus praise his mother or rebuke his mother for her interference at Cana?
- Why are we called to "trust" and "give ourselves" to Mary? How is this different than faith and worship? Doesn't Peter say to entrust our souls to the Creator? Where does Peter tell us to entrust our souls to Mary in the Bible?
- Is mercy referred to by the Bible as coming from Mary? Where does the Bible refer to Mary as the "All-holy" one?
- **Do these claims and titles about Mary elevate her to the level of deity (being a god/goddess)?**
- **Where does the Bible address Mary as the "cause of salvation" (CCC 494)?**
- **Where does the Bible connect Mary to Eve (CCC 494) as it connects Jesus to Adam (1 Cor 15:45)?**
- How do "our prayers" cooperate with Mary to "deliver our souls from death" (CCC 966)? Where does the Bible describe this practice?

WAS MARY A VIRGIN HER ENTIRE LIFE? DID JESUS HAVE ANY BROTHERS?

Passages of The Catechism of the Catholic Church to Consider:

- **"led the Church to confess Mary's real and perpetual virginity" (CCC 499)**
- "Against this doctrine the objection is raise that the Bible mentions brother and sisters of Jesus. The Church has always understood these passages as not referring to other children of the Virgin Mary. In fact James and Joseph, 'brothers of Jesus,' are **sons of another Mary**, a disciple of Christ, whom St. Matthew significantly calls 'the other Mary.' They are **close relations of Jesus**, according to an Old Testament expression." (CCC 500)
- "Mary 'remained a virgin in conceiving her Son, a virgin in giving birth to him, a virgin in carrying him, a virgin in nursing him at her breast, **always a virgin**'" (CCC 510)

Scriptures to Consider:

- Matthew 1:24–25 "When Joseph woke from sleep, he did as the angel of the Lord commanded him: he took his wife, but **knew her not until she had given birth** to a son. And he called his name Jesus." (ESV)

- 1 Corinthians 7:3–5 "The husband should give to his wife her conjugal rights, and **likewise the wife to her husband. [4] For the wife does not have authority over her own body, but the husband does.** Likewise the husband does not have authority over his own body, but the wife does. [5] **Do not deprive one another**, except perhaps by agreement for a limited time, that you may devote yourselves to prayer; but then come together again, so that Satan may not tempt you because of your lack of self-control." (ESV)

- John 7:3–5 "So **his brothers said to him**, "Leave here and go to Judea, that your disciples also may see the works you are doing. [4] For no one works in secret if he seeks to be known openly. If you do these things, show yourself to the world." [5] For not even his brothers believed in him. (ESV)

- Matthew 13:55–56 "Is not this the carpenter's son? **Is not his mother called Mary? And are not his brothers James and Joseph and Simon and Judas? [56] And are not all his sisters with us?** Where then did this man get all these things?" (ESV)

- Luke 8:19–21 "Then **his mother and his brothers came to him**, but they could not reach him because of the crowd. [20] And he was told, "Your mother and your brothers are standing outside, desiring to see you." [21] But he answered them, "My mother and my brothers are those who hear the word of God and do it." (ESV)

- John 2:12 "After this he went down to Capernaum, with his mother and his brothers and his disciples, and they stayed there for a few days." (ESV)

- John 7:5 "For **not even his brothers believed in him.**" (ESV)

- Acts 1:13–14 "And when they had entered, they went up to the upper room, where they were staying, Peter and John and James and Andrew, Philip and Thomas, Bartholomew and Matthew, James the son of Alphaeus and Simon the Zealot and Judas the son of James. [14] All these with one accord were

devoting themselves to prayer, together with the women and **Mary the mother of Jesus, and his brothers**." (ESV)
- 1 Corinthians 9:5 "Do we not have the right to take along a believing wife, as do the other apostles and **the brothers of the Lord** and Cephas?" (ESV)
- 1 Corinthians 15:7 "Then he appeared to James, then to all the apostles." (ESV)
- Galatians 1:19 "But I saw none of the other apostles except **James the Lord's brother**." (ESV)
- Galatians 2:9 "and when James and Cephas and John, who seemed to be pillars, perceived the grace that was given to me, they gave the right hand of fellowship to Barnabas and me, that we should go to the Gentiles and they to the circumcised." (ESV)
- Jude 1 "Jude, a servant of Jesus Christ and **brother of James**"
- James 2:1 "My brothers, show no partiality as you hold the faith in our Lord Jesus Christ, the Lord of glory." (ESV)
- John 2:12 "After this he went down to Capernaum, with his mother and his brothers and his disciples, and they stayed there for a few days." (ESV)

Questions to Consider:
- Would having other children detract from Mary's holiness? Or add to it according to Gen 1:28?
- Genesis 1:28 "And God blessed them. And God said to them, "Be fruitful and multiply and fill the earth and subdue it, and have dominion over the fish of the sea and over the birds of the heavens and over every living thing that moves on the earth." (ESV)
- 1 Timothy 5:14 "So I would have younger widows marry, bear children, manage their households, and give the adversary no occasion for slander." (ESV)
- In John 2, Jesus has just performed a miracle changing water to wine and rebuked his mother Mary in the process. This

same passage refers to Jesus' mother and "brothers" as continuing with him to Capernaum. **Why are these "brothers" referenced and so involved in traveling with Jesus' mother if they are only cousins or more distant relatives?**

- Why is there no historical or linguistic evidence that the Greek words (adelphoi ("brothers") and adelphai ("sisters")) support this idea of them not being brothers and sisters but just distant relatives?
- Would Mary not have been a bad wife is she refused to be physically intimate with her husband Joseph?
  - 1 Corinthians 7:3–5 "The husband should give to his wife her conjugal rights, and likewise the wife to her husband. [4] For the wife does not have authority over her own body, but the husband does. Likewise the husband does not have authority over his own body, but the wife does. [5] Do not deprive one another, except perhaps by agreement for a limited time, that you may devote yourselves to prayer; but then come together again, so that Satan may not tempt you because of your lack of self-control." (ESV)
- Why would the Catholic Church invent and propagate the idea that Mary was always a virgin? If they would twist the Scriptures to misrepresent this, what other areas of their Tradition are untrustworthy?

IS IT TRUE THAT MARY NEVER DIED?

*Passages of The Catechism of the
Catholic Church to Consider:*

- "the Immaculate Virgin...was **taken up body and soul into heavenly glory, and exalted by the Lord as Queen over all things.**" (CCC 966)
- "**she shares in the glory of her Son's Resurrection**, anticipating the resurrection of all members of his Body" (CCC 974)
- "But while in the most Blessed Virgin the Church **has already reached that perfection** whereby she exists without spot or wrinkle, the faithful still strive to conquer sin and increase in holiness. And so they turn their eyes to Mary: in her, the Church is already 'all-holy'" (CCC 829)

Scriptures to Consider:

- Acts 2:32–36 "**This Jesus God raised up**, and of that we all are witnesses. [33] Being therefore exalted at the right hand of God, and having received from the Father the promise of the Holy Spirit, he has poured out this that you yourselves are seeing and hearing. [34] For **David did not ascend into the heavens**, but he himself says, 'The Lord said to my Lord, 'Sit at my right hand, [35] until I make your enemies your footstool.' [36] Let all the house of Israel therefore know for certain that God has made him both Lord and Christ, this Jesus whom you crucified." (ESV)

- 2 Kings 2:10–12 "And he said, "You have asked a hard thing; yet, if you see me as I am being taken from you, it shall be so for you, but if you do not see me, it shall not be so." [11] And as they still went on and talked, behold, chariots of fire and horses of fire separated the two of them. And **Elijah went up by a whirlwind into heaven**. [12] And Elisha saw it and he cried, "My father, my father! The chariots of Israel and its horsemen!" And he saw him no more. Then he took hold of his own clothes and tore them in two pieces." (ESV)
- Genesis 5:23–24 "Thus all the days of Enoch were 365 years. [24] Enoch walked with God, and he was not, for God took him." (ESV)
- Hebrews 11:5 "By faith **Enoch was taken up so that he should not see death**, and he was not found, because God had taken him. Now before he was taken he was commended as having pleased God." (ESV)
- Proverbs 30:6 "Do not add to his words, lest he rebuke you and you be found a liar." (ESV)

Questions to Consider:

- Where does the Bible reference Mary as a Queen?
- Who are the only three people that the Bible references as going directly to Heaven without dying? Why is there such clear evidence and observation about their ascensions?
- Why would the Bible not reference Mary as ascending directly to Heaven also? Who observed it happening? Where is it described?
- When was this idea added to church Tradition? Why did not the apostles or early church fathers speak of this happening with Mary?
- If such a significant claim is made by the Catholic Church, without biblical or early church evidence, is the Catholic Church trustworthy on other issues?

ARE IMAGES AND STATUES OF JESUS, SAINTS, ANGELS, OR MARY HELPFUL OR HARMFUL? DO RELICS AND ROSARIES HAVE SPIRITUAL POWER?

Merriam-Webster's

Definitions to Consider:

How similar are these terms?
Icon - "an object of uncritical devotion; a religious image usually painted on a small wooden panel"
Idol - "an object of extreme devotion; a greatly loved or admired person; a picture or object that is worshipped as a god"

Passages of The Catechism of the Catholic Church to Consider:

- "in the Old Testament, God ordained or permitted the making of images that pointed symbolically toward salvation by the incarnate Word; so it was with the bronze serpent, the ark of the covenant, and the cherubim" (CCC 2129)

- "the Christian veneration of images is not contrary to the first commandment which proscribes idols. ... 'whoever venerates an image venerates the person portrayed in it.' The honor paid to the sacred image is a 'respectful veneration,' not the adoration due to God alone" (CCC 2132)

- "The veneration of sacred images is based on the mystery of the Incarnation of the Word of God. **It is not contrary to the first commandment**." (CCC 2141)

- "Previously God, who has neither a body nor a face, absolutely could not be represented by an image. But now that he has made himself visible in the flesh and has lived with men, **I can make an image of what I have seen of God** ... and contemplate the glory of the Lord, his face unveiled" (CCC 1159)

- "sacred images of the holy Mother of God and of the saints... truly signify Christ, who is glorifies in them...they make manifest the 'cloud of witnesses' who continue to participate in the salvation of the world and to whom we are united...so too are the angels" (CCC 1161)

- "'Following the divinely inspired teachings of our holy Fathers and the tradition of the Catholic Church (for we know that this tradition comes from the Holy Spirit who dwells in her) ...**holy images of our Lord and God and Savior, Jesus Christ, our inviolate Lady, the holy Mother of God, and the venerated angels, all the saints and the just, whether painted or made of mosaic or another suitable material, are to be exhibited in the holy churches of God, on sacred vessels and vestments, walls and panels, in houses and on streets**" (CCC 1161)

Merriam-Webster's

Definitions to Consider:

Amulet - a small object worn to protect the person wearing it

against bad things (such as illness, bad luck, etc.)
Charm - something worn about the person to ward off evil or ensure good fortune
Fetish - an object of irrational reverence or obsessive devotion

Passages of The Catechism of the Catholic Church to Consider:

- **"Medieval piety in the West developed the prayer of the rosary"** (CCC 2678)
- "Christian prayer tries above all to meditate on the mysteries of Christ, as in *lector divine* or the rosary" (CCC 2708)
- "The liturgical feasts dedicated to the Mother of God and Marian prayer, such as **the rosary, an 'epitome of the whole Gospel,' express this devotion to the Virgin Mary.**" (CCC 971)
- **"sacramentals...prepare us to receive grace and dispose us to cooperate with it"** (CCC 1670)
- "from the Paschal mystery of the Passion, Death, and Resurrection of Christ...all sacraments and sacramentals draw their power. There is scarcely any proper use of material things which cannot be thus directed toward the sanctification of men and the praise of God" (CCC 1670)
- "among sacramentals, blessings (of persons, meals, objects, and places) come first" (CCC 1671)

Scriptures to Consider:

- 2 Kings 18:4–6 And **he broke in pieces the bronze serpent** that Moses had made, for until those days **the people of Israel had made offerings to it** (it was called Nehushtan). [5] He trusted in the LORD, the God of Israel, so that there was none like him among all the kings of Judah after him, nor among those who were before him. [6] For he held fast to the LORD. He did not depart from following him, but kept the commandments that the LORD commanded Moses." (ESV)

- Jeremiah 3:16–17 "And when you have multiplied and been fruitful in the land, in those days, declares the LORD, they shall no more say, "The ark of the covenant of the LORD." It shall not come to mind or be remembered or missed; it shall not be made again. [17] At that time Jerusalem shall be called the throne of the LORD, and all nations shall gather to it, to the presence of the LORD in Jerusalem, and they shall no more stubbornly follow their own evil heart." (ESV)
- Revelation 11:19 "Then God's temple in heaven was opened, and the ark of his covenant was seen within his temple."
- Exodus 20:4–5 "**You shall not make for yourself a carved image, or any likeness of anything that is in heaven above, or that is in the earth beneath**, or that is in the water under the earth. [5] You shall not bow down to them or serve them, for I the LORD your God am a jealous God, visiting the iniquity of the fathers on the children to the third and the fourth generation of those who hate me" (ESV)
- **Why does the Catholic Church combine the 2nd & 1st commandment into just the "first" commandment & then split out the 10th commandment into two?** (CCC 2051)
- Deuteronomy 5:8–10 "'You shall not make for yourself a carved image, or any likeness of anything that is in heaven above, or that is on the earth beneath, or that is in the water under the earth. [9] You shall not bow down to them or serve them; for I the LORD your God am a jealous God, visiting the iniquity of the fathers on the children to the third and fourth generation of those who hate me, [10] but showing steadfast love to thousands of those who love me and keep my commandments." (ESV)
- Leviticus 26:1 "You shall not make idols for yourselves or erect an image or pillar, and you shall not set up a figured stone in your land to bow down to it, for I am the LORD your God." (ESV)
- Deuteronomy 4:16–19 "beware lest you act corruptly by making a carved image for yourselves, in the **form of any figure, the likeness of male or female**, [17] the likeness of any animal

that is on the earth, the likeness of any winged bird that flies in the air, [18] the likeness of anything that creeps on the ground, the likeness of any fish that is in the water under the earth. [19] And beware lest you raise your eyes to heaven, and when you see the sun and the moon and the stars, all the host of heaven, you be drawn away and bow down to them and serve them, things that the LORD your God has allotted to all the peoples under the whole heaven." (ESV)

- Micah 5:13 "and I will cut off your carved images and your pillars from among you, and you shall bow down no more to the work of your hands" (ESV)
- Psalm 97:7 "All worshipers of images are put to shame, who make their boast in worthless idols; worship him, all you gods!" (ESV)
- Ezekiel 7:20 "His beautiful ornament they used for pride, and they made their abominable images and their detestable things of it. Therefore I make it an unclean thing to them." (ESV)
- Habakkuk 2:18–20 "What profit is an idol when its maker has shaped it, a metal image, a teacher of lies? For its maker trusts in his own creation when he makes speechless idols! [19] Woe to him who says to a wooden thing, Awake; to a silent stone, Arise! Can this teach?Behold, it is overlaid with gold and silver, and there is no breath at all in it. [20] But the LORD is in his holy temple; let all the earth keep silence before him." (ESV)
- Isaiah 2:8 "Their land is filled with idols; **they bow down to the work of their hands**, to what their own fingers have made." (ESV)
- Acts 17:29 "Being then God's offspring, **we ought not to think that the divine being is like gold or silver or stone, an image formed by the art and imagination of man**." (ESV)
- Colossians 2:18 "Let no one disqualify you, **insisting on** asceticism and **worship of angels**, going on in detail about visions, puffed up without reason by his sensuous mind" (ESV)
- Revelation 13:14 "and by the signs that it is allowed to work in the presence of the beast it deceives those who dwell on earth, telling them to make an image for the beast that was wounded

by the sword and yet lived." (ESV)
- Revelation 22:8–9 "I, John, am the one who heard and saw these things. And when I heard and saw them, I fell down to worship at the feet of the angel who showed them to me, [9] but he said to me, "**You must not do that!** I am a fellow servant with you and your brothers the prophets, and with those who keep the words of this book. Worship God." (ESV)
- Romans 1:22–25 "Claiming to be wise, they became fools, [23] and **exchanged the glory of the immortal God for images resembling mortal man** and birds and animals and creeping things. [24] Therefore God gave them up in the lusts of their hearts to impurity, to the dishonoring of their bodies among themselves, [25] because they exchanged the truth about God for a lie and worshiped and served the creature rather than the Creator, who is blessed forever! Amen. (ESV)
- Ezekiel 13:20–21 "Therefore thus says the Lord GOD: Behold, I am against your magic bands with which you hunt the souls like birds, and I will tear them from your arms, and I will let the souls whom you hunt go free, the souls like birds. [21] Your veils also I will tear off and deliver my people out of your hand, and they shall be no more in your hand as prey, and you shall know that I am the LORD. (ESV)
- Psalm 20:7 "Some trust in chariots and some in horses, but we trust in the name of the LORD our God." (ESV)
- Acts 5:15 "so that they even carried out the sick into the streets and laid them on cots and mats, that as Peter came by at least his shadow might fall on some of them." (ESV)
- Acts 19:11–12 "And God was doing extraordinary miracles by the hands of Paul, [12] so that even handkerchiefs or aprons that had touched his skin were carried away to the sick, and their diseases left them and the evil spirits came out of them." (ESV)
- Acts 19:19 "And a number of those who had practiced magic arts brought their books together and burned them in the sight of all. And they counted the value of them and found it came to fifty thousand pieces of silver." (ESV)

- Mark 5:28 "For she said, 'If I touch even his garments, I will be made well.'" (ESV)
- Mark 5:34 "And he said to her, 'Daughter, your faith has made you well; go in peace, and be healed of your disease.'" (ESV)

Questions to Consider:

- If objects from the Old Testament such as the bronze serpent, the ark of the covenant, and the cherubim were so important for our faith, why do we not have them today?
- **Why did King Hezekiah destroy the bronze serpent in 2 Kings 18:4? How does verses 5 & 6 describe King Hezekiah?**
- **Why is the ark of the covenant now in Heaven and not on earth? (Revelation 11:19)**
- **What does Acts 19:19 teach us about dangers that can be found in objects? When should we get rid of or destroy objects? Why is trust the critical issue?**
- Why did the early church father Eusebius warn against amulets being dangerous? **When can an object like a rosary, relic, statue, or image become more like an amulet in our hearts?**
- Why did people use objects as idols in the Bible? What were they trying to gain? What were they trying to get rid of? When can an object become an idol in our hearts today?
- Why are we warned about putting our trust in objects like horses and chariots (military might) for protection from evil?
- In Acts 5:15-16 was the healing from the proximity to Peter, or from the faith in the Spirit of the Living God that caused them to draw near to Jesus within Peter?
- Did the woman's proximity to Jesus heal her? Did the woman's touching of Jesus heal her? Or was it her faith? Objects and proximity to objects are not needed. Faith in Jesus is what is needed.
- In John 5:1–11 at the Pool of Bethesda Jesus does not choose to heal everyone. Why not?
- Why doesn't Jesus, Peter, or Paul require an offering in return for the healing that came? **Is it wrong for the Church to collect**

offerings in conjunction with healings?

- SEE: "What Does the Bible Say about Idols?"
  www.trustworthyword.com/idols

SHOULD WE PRAY TO MARY AND SAINTS?

Merriam-Webster's Definitions:

Necromancy - the practice of talking to the spirits of dead people

Medium - a person through whom other persons try to communicate with the spirits of the dead

Passages of The Catechism of the Catholic Church to Consider:

- **"We can pray with and to her.** The prayer of the Church is sustained by the prayer of Mary" (CCC 2679)
- "prayer unites us in the Church with the Mother of Jesus" (CCC 2673)
- "the Churches developed their prayers to the holy Mother of God" (CCC 2675)
- "in countless hymns and antiphons expressing this prayer... entrusts the supplications and praises of the children of God to the Mother of Jesus" (CCC 2675)
- "we can entrust all our cares and petitions to her: she prays for us" (CCCC 2677)
- "by entrusting ourselves to her prayer we abandon ourselves to the will of God together with her" (CCC 2677)
- "Medieval piety in the West developed the prayer of the rosary" (CCC 2678)
- "Mary is the perfect Orans (pray-er)" (CCC 2679)

- "The witnesses...especially those whom the Church recognizes as saints...constantly care for those whom have left on the earth. Their intercession is their most exalted service to God's plan. **We can and should ask them to intercede for us and for the whole world.**" (CCC 2683)
- "it is a holy and wholesome thought **to pray for the dead** that they may be loosed from their sins' she offers suffrages for them" (CCC 958)
- "prayer is the raising of one's mind and heart to God or the requesting of good things from God" (CCC 2559)
- Where is confessing to God?
- "In prayer, the pilgrim Church is associated with that of **the saints, whose intercession she asks**" (CCC 2692)
- **"it is a holy and wholesome thought to pray for the dead that they may be loosed from their sins' she offers suffrages for them" (CCC 958)**
- "The Church encourages us to prepare ourselves for the house of death. ... **to ask the Mother of God to intercede for us** 'at the hour of our death' in the *Hail Mary;* and **to entrust ourselves to St. Joseph**, the patron of a happy death" (CCC 1014)
- "This teaching is also based on the practice of prayer for the dead, already mentioned in Sacred Scripture: 'Therefore [Judas Maccabeus] made atonement for the dead, that they might be delivered from sin." (CCC 1032)
- "The Christian funeral...aims at expressing efficacious communion with the deceased" (CCC 1684)
- "The Church...asks [to the Father] to purify his child of his sins and their consequences and to admit him to the Paschal fullness of the table of the Kingdom. ... by communicating the Body of Christ...by praying for him and with him." (CCC)
- "saints...constantly care for those whom they have left on earth...their intercession is their most exalted service to God's plan. We can and should ask them to intercede for us and for the whole world." (CCC 2683)
- "the Church...sustains the hope of believers by proposing the saints to them as models and **intercessors**" (CCC 828)

Scriptures to Consider:

- Deuteronomy 18:10–12 "There shall not be found among you…a medium or a necromancer or one who inquires of the dead, for whoever does these things is an abomination to the LORD. And because of these abominations the LORD your God is driving them out before you." (ESV)
- Leviticus 19:31 "Do not turn to mediums or necromancers; do not seek them out, and so make yourselves unclean by them: I am the LORD your God." (ESV)
- Isaiah 8:19 "And when they say to you, 'Inquire of the mediums and the necromancers who chirp and mutter,' **should not a people inquire of their God? Should they inquire of the dead on behalf of the living**?'" (ESV)
- 1 Samuel 28:15 "Then Samuel said to Saul, "**Why have you disturbed me** by bringing me up?" Saul answered, "I am in great distress, for the Philistines are warring against me, and God has turned away from me and answers me no more, either by prophets or by dreams. Therefore I have summoned you to tell me what I shall do." (ESV)
- 1 Chronicles 10:13–14 "So Saul died for his breach of faith. He broke faith with the LORD in that he did not keep the command of the LORD, and also [14] **He did not seek guidance from the LORD**. Therefore the LORD put him to death and turned the kingdom over to David the son of Jesse." (ESV)
- Isaiah 45:20 "Assemble yourselves and come; draw near together, you survivors of the nations! They have no knowledge who carry about their wooden idols, and keep on praying to a god that cannot save." (ESV)
- Hebrews 7:27 "He has no need, like those high priests, to offer sacrifices daily, first for his own sins and then for those of the people, since he did this once for all when he offered up himself." (ESV)
- James 1:5 "If any of you lacks wisdom, let him ask God, who

gives generously to all without reproach, and it will be given him." (ESV)

- Romans 8:26–27 "Likewise the Spirit helps us in our weakness. For we do not know what to pray for as we ought, but the **Spirit himself intercedes for us** with groanings too deep for words. [27] And he who searches hearts knows what is the mind of the Spirit, because the Spirit intercedes for the saints according to the will of God." (ESV)
- Romans 8:34 "Christ Jesus is the one who died—more than that, who was raised—who is at the right hand of God, who indeed is interceding for us." (ESV)

IS IT OK TO PRAY
TO ANGELS?

Passages of The Catechism of the Catholic Church to Consider:

- "the Church...invokes their [the angels] assistance in the funeral...'May the angels lead you into Paradise...she celebrates the memory of certain angels more particularly ? (St. Michael, St. Gabriel, St. Raphael, and the guardian angels'" (CCC 335)
- "Beside each believer stands an angel as protector and shepherd leading him to life" (CCC 336)
- **"The Church venerates the angels** who help her on her earthly pilgrimage and protect every human being." (CCC 352)

Scriptures to Consider:

- NOTE: The Bible does not mention Raphael or particular "guardian" angels assigned to each believe nor does it support praying to them for assistance as prayer is an act of worship and angels refuse worship.
- Why does the book of Tobit give so much attention to angels compared with every other book of the Bible? Does that concern you about its trustworthiness? Should it?
- Revelation 22:8–9 "I, John, am the one who heard and saw these things. And when I heard and saw them, I fell down to worship at the feet of the angel who showed them to me, [9] but he said to me, "You must not do that! I am a fellow servant with you and your brothers the prophets, and with those who

keep the words of this book. Worship God." (ESV)

- Colossians 2:16–19 "Therefore let no one pass judgment on you in questions of food and drink, or with regard to a festival or a new moon or a Sabbath. [17] These are a shadow of the things to come, but the substance belongs to Christ. [18] Let no one disqualify you, *insisting on* asceticism and *worship of angels*, going on in detail about visions, puffed up without reason by his sensuous mind, [19] and not holding fast to the Head, from whom the whole body, nourished and knit together through its joints and ligaments, grows with a growth that is from God." (ESV)
- Hebrews 13:5 "he has said, 'I will never leave you nor forsake you.'" (ESV)
- Romans 1:22–25 "Claiming to be wise, they became fools, [23] and exchanged the glory of the immortal God for images resembling mortal man and birds and animals and creeping things. [24] Therefore God gave them up in the lusts of their hearts to impurity, to the dishonoring of their bodies among themselves, [25] because they exchanged the truth about God for a lie and **worshiped and served the creature rather than the Creator,** who is blessed forever! Amen." (ESV)

Questions to Consider:

- Where does the Bible describe or prescribe praying to Mary, Saints, or Angels?
- Why would we talk to angels when we have the Spirit of God within us, to whom we can speak at anytime? Is not the God the Holy Spirit more powerful than angels?
- **Is it not insulting to ignore the Holy Spirit (whose job is to intercede for us) and instead speak to created beings rather than the Creator?**
- Where does the Bible say that every believer have an individual angel assigned to them?
- How is praying to unseen spiritual beings not a form of

worship?

- Where does the Bible describe the dead as praying for the living?
- Is talking to the dead (Mary and Saints) in prayer any different than necromancy? Why or why not?
- **Why does God give so many warnings about necromancy and mediums like in Isaiah 8:19?**
- **Why was Saul's sin "that he did not seek guidance from the Lord" directly so serious? (1 Chronicles 10:13–14)**
- **When was prayer to Mary, the saints, and angels invented by the Catholic Church? Why?**

WILL I GO TO PURGATORY?

Passages of The Catechism of the Catholic Church to Consider:

- "Woe on those who will die in mortal sin!" (CCC 1014)
- "Grave sin deprives us of communion with God and therefore makes us incapable of eternal life" (CCC 1472)
- "every sin, even venial, entails an unhealthy attachment to creatures, **which must be purified here on earth, or after death in a state called Purgatory**" (CCC 1472)
- "this purification frees one from what is called the 'temporal punishment' of sin" (CCC 1472)
- "A conversion which proceeds from a fervent charity can attain the complete purification of the sinner in such a way that no punishment would remain" (CCC 1472)
- "Each man receives his eternal retribution in his immortal soul at the very moment of his death, in a particular judgment that refers his life to Christ: either entrance into the blessedness of heaven - **through purification** or immediately, or immediate and everlasting damnation. 'At the evening of life we shall be judged on our love." (CCC 1022)
- "the souls of all the saints...and other faithful who died after receiving Christ's holy Baptism (provided they were not in need of purification when they died, ... or, if they then did need or will need some purification, when they have been purified after death, ...)...will be in heaven" (CCC 1023)
- "All who died in God's grace and friendship, but are still

imperfectly purified, are indeed assured of their eternal salvation; but after death they **undergo purification, so as to achieve the holiness necessary to enter the joy of heaven**" (CCC 1030)

- "The Church gives the name *Purgatory* to this final purification of the elect, which is entirely different from the punishment of the damned" (CCC 1031)
- **"The Church formulated their doctrine of faith on Purgatory especially at the Councils of Florence [1439] and Trent [1563].** The tradition of the Church, by reference to certain texts of Scripture, speaks of a cleansing fire." (CCC 1031)
- "for certain lesser faults, we must believe that, before the Final Judgment, there is a purifying fire" (CCC 1031)
- **"we understand that certain offenses can be forgiven in this age, but certain others in the age to come"** (CCC 1031)
- "From the beginning the Church has honored the memory of the dead and offered prayers in suffrage for them, above all the Eucharistic sacrifice, so that, thus purified, they may attain the beatific vision of God" (CCC 1032)
- **"The Church also commends almsgiving, indulgences, and works of penance undertaken on behalf of the dead"** (CCC 1032)
- **"Let us not hesitate to help those who have died and to offer our prayers for them"** (CCC 1032)

DO INDULGENCES HELP US?

Passages of The Catechism of the Catholic Church to Consider:

- "An indulgence is a remission before God of the temporal punishment due to sins whose guilt has already been forgiven, which the faithful Christian who is duly disposed gains under certain prescribed conditions throughout the action of the Church which, as the minister of redemption dispenses and applies with authority the treasury of the satisfactions of Christ and the saints" (CCC 1471)
- "relatives who must see to it that the sick receive at the proper time the sacraments that prepare them to meet the living God" (CCC 2299)
- **"An indulgence...removes either part or all of the temporal punishment due to sin. The faithful can gain indulgences for themselves or apply them to the dead." (CCC 1471)**
- "every sin, even venial, entails an unhealthy attachment to creates, which must be purified either here on earth, or after death, in the state called Purgatory" (CCC 1472)
- "a perennial link of charity exists between the faithful who have already reached their heavenly home, those who are expiating their sins in purgatory, and those who are still pilgrims on earth. Between theme there is, too, and abundant exchange of good things.' In this wonderful exchange the holiness of one profits others, well beyond the harm that the sin of one could cause others. Thus recourse to the communion of saints lets

the contrite sinner be more promptly and efficaciously purified for the punishments for sin" (CCC 1475)

- **"This treasury includes as well the prayers and good works of the Blessed Virgin Mary" (CCC 1477)**
- **"In this treasury too, are the prayers and good works of all the saints" (CCC 1477)**
- **"In this way they attained their own salvation and at the same time cooperated in saving their brothers" (CCC 1477)**
- "Since the faithful departed now being purified are also members of the same communion of saints, one way we can help them is to obtain indulgences for them so that the temporal punishments for their sins may be remitted" (CCC 1479)
- "Through indulgences the faithful can obtain the remission of temporal punishment resulting from sin for themselves and also for the souls in Purgatory" (CCC 1498)
- 2 Maccabbees 12:43, "And making a gathering, he sent twelve thousand drachms of silver to Jerusalem for sacrifice to be offered for the sins of the dead, thinking well and religiously concerning the resurrection."

Scriptures to Consider:

- 1 John 2:2 "He is the propitiation for our sins, and not for ours only but also for the sins of the whole world." (ESV)
- Romans 5:8 "God shows his love for us in that while we were still sinners, Christ died for us."
- 1 Corinthians 13:15 "If anyone's work is burned up, he will suffer loss, though he himself will be saved, but only as through fire." (ESV)
- 1 Peter 1:7 "so that the tested genuineness of your faith—more precious than gold that perishes though it is tested by fire—may be found to result in praise and glory and honor at the revelation of Jesus Christ." (ESV)
- Hebrews 7:27 "He has no need, like those high priests, to offer sacrifices daily, first for his own sins and then for those

of the people, since he did this once for all when he offered up himself." (ESV)

- 2 Corinthians 5:6-8 "So we are always of good courage. We know that while we are at home in the body we are away from the Lord, 7 for we walk by faith, not by sight. 8 Yes, we are of good courage, and **we would rather be away from the body and at home with the Lord**." (ESV)
- Philippians 1:21 "For to me to live is Christ, and to die is gain." (ESV)
- **Philippians 1:23 "My desire is to depart and be with Christ, for that is far better."**
- Job 1:5 "And when the days of the feast had run their course, Job would send and consecrate them, and he would rise early in the morning and offer burnt offerings according to the number of them all. For Job said, 'It may be that my children have sinned, and cursed God in their hearts." Thus Job did continually.'" (ESV)
- Luke 23:43 "Truly, I say to you, **today** you will be with me in **paradise**." (ESV)
- Deuteronomy 4:2 "You shall not add to the word that I command you, nor take from it, that you may keep the commandments of the LORD your God that I command you." (ESV)
- Romans 8:1–2 "There is therefore now no condemnation for those who are in Christ Jesus. [2] For the law of the Spirit of life has set you free in Christ Jesus from the law of sin and death." (ESV)
- 1 John 1:9 "If we confess our sins, he is faithful and just to forgive us our sins and to cleanse us from all unrighteousness." (ESV)
- Colossians 2:13–14 "And you, who were dead in your trespasses and the uncircumcision of your flesh, God made alive together with him, having forgiven us all our trespasses, [14] by canceling the record of debt that stood against us with its legal demands. This he set aside, nailing it to the cross." (ESV)

Questions to consider:

- Were Job's sons alive or dead when made offerings for them (Job 1:5)?
- **Does 1 Corinthians 13:14-15 speak about people being burned up or their works being burned up to evidence their quality/genuineness? Does it talk about the person being burned or escaping from the fire or being cleansed by the fire?**
- **If the Bible speaks so much about Heaven and Hell, why did it take the Catholic Church 1400+ years to approve a statement on Purgatory?**
  - "The Church formulated their doctrine of faith on Purgatory especially at the Councils of Florence [1439 A.D.] and Trent [1563 A.D.]." (CCC 1031)
- What were the motives of the Catholic doctrine of Purgatory? How were they connected with indulgences and money/fundraising? Why were Martin Luther and other reformers so much against this abuse of power and manipulative tactics?
- **Why does the Bible have so many warnings about adding to it?** What is the danger? What is the offense? How has the Catholic Church offended God in the invention of purgatory?
- **Where is the concept of indulgences in the Bible?**
- What does Romans 8:1-2 mean? What does 1 John 1:9 mean?
- If our debt has been fully paid (Colossians 2:13–14), why is there a need for Purgatory or Indulgences?
- SEE: "What Does the Bible Say About Heaven?" www.trustworthyword.com/what-does-the-bible-say-about-heaven
- SEE: "What Does the Bible Say About Hell?" www.trustworthyword.com/what-does-the-bible-say-about-hell

CAN MARRIAGES BE ANNULLED? WHAT ABOUT REMARRIAGE?

Passages of The Catechism of the Catholic Church to Consider:

- "The Church, after an examination of the situation by the competent ecclesiastical tribunal can declare the nullity of a marriage, i.e., **that the marriage never existed**. In this case the contracting parties are free to marry, provided the natural obligations of a previous union are discharged." (CCC 1629)
- "A case of marriage with disparity of cult (**between a Catholic and a non-baptized person**) requires even greater circumspection" (1633)
- "In the case of disparity of cult an express dispensation from this impediment is required for the validity of the marriage. (1635)
- "the remarriage of persons divorced from a living, lawful spouse contravenes the plan and law of God as taught by Christ. They are not separated from the Church, but *they cannot receive Eucharistic communion.*" (CCC 1665)
- [Encouragement to divorce if your wife does not obey you] Sirach 25:35-36 "If she walk not at thy hand, she will confound thee in the sight of thy enemies. 36 Cut her off from thy flesh, lest she always abuse thee."

Scriptures to Consider:

- Mark 10:7–9 'Therefore a man shall leave his father and mother and hold fast to his wife, [8] and the two shall become one flesh. 'So they are no longer two but one flesh. [9] What therefore God has joined together, let not man separate." (ESV)
- Romans 7:2–3 "For a married woman is bound by law to her husband while he lives, but if her husband dies she is released from the law of marriage. [3] Accordingly, she will be called an adulteress if she lives with another man while her husband is alive. But if her husband dies, she is free from that law, and if she marries another man she is not an adulteress." (ESV)
- 1 Corinthians 7:39 "A wife is bound to her husband as long as he lives. But if her husband dies, she is free to be married to whom she wishes, only in the Lord." (ESV)
- SEE: "What Does the Bible Say about Divorce and Remarriage?" www.trustworthyword.com/what-does-the-bible-say-about-divorce-and-remarriage

Questions to Consider:

- Is the concept of "annulment" (that a "marriage never existed") a biblical concept? If so, where?
- How does that differ with Romans 7:2 and 1 Corinthians 7:39 saying that only death ends a marriage?
- Does the Bible ever distinguish between marriages inside or outside the church?
- Is it right to provide an avenue of allow marriage to a non-believer when the Bible prohibits it clearly (1 Corinthians 7:39)?
- Is not withholding Eucharistic communion withholding forgiveness?
- Why would Sirach 25:35-36 encourage divorce in such a sweeping manner? Does the Bible encourage it or permit it on rare occasions?

WHO WILL GO TO HEAVEN?

INTERNAL INCONSISTENCIES IN THE CATECHISM OF THE CATHOLIC CHURCH

Exclusivism VS. Inclusivism/ Pluralism/Universalism Definitions

Religious Exclusivism - doctrine or belief that only one particular religion or belief system is true

Religious Inclusivism - Jesus 'death also provide salvation for some who do not believe, salvation for people apart from conscious faith in Christ, but still only through Jesus; followers of other religions and even atheists can be saved by responding to God's general revelation

Religious Pluralism - acceptance of the concept that two or more religions with mutually exclusive truth claims are equally valid

Religious Universalism - a theological doctrine that all human beings will eventually be saved

Religious Syncretism - blending of two or more religious belief systems into a new system

The -Ism Differences

Exclusivism - only one way, requires a response
Is Jesus the only way? YES
Do you have to respond? YES

Inclusivism - general revelation saves, must be sincere
Is Jesus the only way? NO
Do you have to respond? YES

Pluralism - many ways to God
Is Jesus the only way? NO
Do you have to respond? NO

Universalism – everyone is going to be saved
Is Jesus the only way? NO
Do you have to respond? NO

Some Catholic claims to Exclusivism in 'The Catechism of the Catholic Church':

- ""The sole Church of Christ [is that] which our Savior, after his Resurrection, entrusted to Peter's pastoral care, commissioning him and the other apostles to extend and rule it. ... This Church, constituted and organized as a society in the present world, subsists in (*subsistit in*) the Catholic Church, which is governed by the successor of Peter and by the bishops in communion with him." (CCC 816)

- "For it is through Christ's Catholic Church alone, which is the universal hope toward salvation, that the fullness of the means of salvation can be obtained" (CCC 816)
- "Just as the office which the Lord confided to Peter alone, as first of the apostles, destined to be transmitted to his successors, is a permanent one, so also endures the office...Hence the Church teaches that 'the bishops have by divine institution taken the place of the apostles as pastors of the Church, in such wise that whoever listens to them is listening to Christ and whoever despises them despises Christ and him who sent Christ" (CCC 862)
- "They could not be saved who, knowing that the Catholic Church was founded as necessary by God through Christ, would refuse to enter it or to remain in it" (CCC 846)
- "The second precept 'You shall confess your sins at least once per year' ensures preparation for the Eucharist by the reception of the sacrament of reconciliation, which continues Baptism's work of conversion and forgiveness" (CCC 2042)
- "No one can have God as Father who does not have the Church as Mother" (CCC 181)
- "Reconciliation with the Church is inseparable from reconciliation with God" (CCC 1445)
- "For it is through Christ's Catholic Church alone, which is the universal hope toward salvation, that the fullness of the means of salvation can be obtained" (CCC 816)
- "It is clear therefore that, in the supremely wise arrangement of God, sacred Tradition, Sacred Scripture, and the Magisterium of the Church are so connected and associated that one of them cannot stand without the others. Working together each in its own way, under the action of the one Holy Spirit, they all contribute effectively to the salvation of souls." (CCC 95)

- "The task of giving an authentic interpretation of the Word of God, whether in its written form or the form of Tradition, has been entrusted to the living, teaching office of the Church alone"(CCC 85)
- "the Father willed to call the whole of humanity together into his Son's Church. The Church is where humanity must rediscover its unity and salvation. The Church is 'the world reconciled.'" (CCC 845)
- **MORAL EXCLUSIVISM vs. MORAL INCLUSIVISM:** "to the Church belongs the right always and everywhere to announce moral principles, including those pertaining to the social order, and to make judgments on any human affairs" (CCC 2032)

Some claims to Inclusivism and Pluralism in The Catechism of the Catholic Church:

A Concerning Inconsistency within the CCC and with the Scripture...
- **PROTESTANTISM:** "All who have been justified by faith in Baptism are incorporated into Christ; they therefore have the right to be called Christians, and with good reason are accepted as brothers in the Lord by the children of the Catholic Church" (CCC 818)
- "Many elements of sanctification and of truth are found outside the visible confines of the Catholic Church...Christ's Spirit uses these Churches and ecclesial communities as a means of salvation" (CCC 819)
- **ISLAM:** "The Church's relationship with the Muslims. 'The plan of salvation also includes those who acknowledge the Creator, in the first place amongst whom are the Muslims; these profess to hold the faith of Abraham, and together with us they adore the one, merciful God, mankind's judge on the

last day." (CCC 841)

- **OTHER RELIGIONS:** "the Catholic Church recognizes in other religions that search, among shadows and images, for God who is unknown yet near...the Church considers all goodness and truth found in these religions as a 'preparation for the Gospel'" (CCC 843)
- **EVERYONE OUTSIDE CATHOLIC EXPOSURE:** "Those, who through no fault of their own, do not know the Gospel of Christ or his church, but nonetheless seek God with a sincere heart, and moved by grace, try in their own actions to do his will as they know it through the dictates of their conscience - those too may achieve eternal salvation" (CCC 847)
- "Every man who is ignorant of the Gospel of Christ and of his Church, but seeks the truth and does the will of God in accordance with his understanding of it, can be saved. It may be supposed that such persons would have desired Baptism explicitly if they had known its necessity" (CCC 1260)
- "those who, without knowing of the Church but acting under the inspiration of grace, seek God sincerely and strive to fulfill his will, can be saved even if they haven't been baptized" (CCC 1280)

Scriptures to Consider:

- 2 Timothy 4:3–4 "For the time is coming when people will not endure sound teaching, but having itching ears they will accumulate for themselves teachers to suit their own passions, [4] and will turn away from listening to the truth and wander off into myths." (ESV)
- 1 Cor 2:5 "so that your faith might not rest in the wisdom of men but in the power of God."

Universal Accountability to God:

- Romans 1:18–23 "For the wrath of God is revealed from heaven against all ungodliness and unrighteousness of men, who by their unrighteousness suppress the truth. [19]

For what can be known about God is plain to them, because God has shown it to them. [20] For his invisible attributes, namely, his eternal power and divine nature, have been clearly perceived, ever since the creation of the world, in the things that have been made. So they are without excuse. [21] For although they knew God, they did not honor him as God or give thanks to him, but they became futile in their thinking, and their foolish hearts were darkened. [22] Claiming to be wise, they became fools, [23] and exchanged the glory of the immortal God for images resembling mortal man and birds and animals and creeping things." (ESV)

- Romans 3:10–12 "as it is written: 'None is righteous, no, not one; no one understands; no one seeks for God. All have turned aside; together they have become worthless; no one does good, not even one." (ESV)
- Romans 5:10–11 "For if while we were enemies we were reconciled to God by the death of his Son, much more, now that we are reconciled, shall we be saved by his life. [11] More than that, we also rejoice in God through our Lord Jesus Christ, through whom we have now received reconciliation." (ESV)
- Joshua 23:16 "if you transgress the covenant of the Lord your God, which he commanded you, and go and serve other gods and bow down to them. Then the anger of the Lord will be kindled against you, and you shall perish quickly from off the good land that he has given to you." (ESV)

God's Inclusive Invitation to All:

- John 3:16 "For God so loved the world, that he gave his only Son, that whoever believes in him should not perish but have eternal life." (ESV)
- 1 Timothy 2:3–5 "This is good, and it is pleasing in the sight of God our Savior, [4] who desires all people to be saved and to come to the knowledge of the truth. [5] For there is one God, and there is one mediator between God and men, the man Christ Jesus" (ESV)

- 2 Peter 3:9 "The Lord is not slow to fulfill his promise as some count slowness, but is patient toward you, not wishing that any should perish, but that all should reach repentance." (ESV)
- Romans 2:4–5 "Or do you presume on the riches of his kindness and forbearance and patience, not knowing that God's kindness is meant to lead you to repentance? [5] But because of your hard and impenitent heart you are storing up wrath for yourself on the day of wrath when God's righteous judgment will be revealed." (ESV)

Salvation is through faith alone in Jesus (exclusive means & response):
- Acts 4:12 "And there is salvation in no one else, for there is no other name under heaven given among men by which we must be saved." (ESV)
- John 14:6 "Jesus said to him, 'I am the way, and the truth, and the life. No one comes to the Father except through me.'" (ESV)
- Romans 10:9–10 "because, if you confess with your mouth that Jesus is Lord and believe in your heart that God raised him from the dead, you will be saved. [10] For with the heart one believes and is justified, and with the mouth one confesses and is saved. (ESV)
- Romans 10:13–15 "For 'everyone who calls on the name of the Lord will be saved.' [14] How then will they call on him in whom they have not believed? And how are they to believe in him of whom they have never heard? And how are they to hear without someone preaching? [15] And how are they to preach unless they are sent? As it is written, 'How beautiful are the feet of those who preach the good news!'" (ESV)
- 2 John 9 "Everyone who goes on ahead and does not abide in the teaching of Christ, does not have God. Whoever abides in the teaching has both the Father and the Son." (ESV)
- 2 Corinthians 5:11 "Therefore, knowing the fear of the Lord, we persuade others. But what we are is known to God, and I

hope it is known also to your conscience." (ESV)
- John 3:3 "Truly, truly, I say to you, unless one is born again he cannot see the kingdom of God."

Proverbs 30:5–6 "Every word of God proves true; he is a shield to those who take refuge in him. Do not add to his words, lest he rebuke you and you be found a liar." (ESV)

WHY IS THE CATHOLIC BIBLE DIFFERENT THAN OTHERS?

IS THE DEUTEROCANON/ APOCRYPHA TRUSTWORTHY?

- "It is clear therefore that, in the supremely wise arrangement of God, sacred Tradition, Sacred Scripture, and the Magisterium of the Church are so connected and associated that one of them cannot stand without the others. Working together each in its own way, under the action of the one Holy Spirit, they all contribute effectively to the salvation of souls." (CCC 95)
- "The task of giving an **authentic interpretation of the Word of God**, whether in its written form or the form of Tradition, has been **entrusted to the living, teaching office of the Church alone**" (CCC 85)
- **"The task of interpreting the Word of God authentically has been entrusted solely to the Magesterium of the Church, that is, to the Pope and to the bishops in communion with him." (CCC 100)**
- "It was by the apostolic Tradition that the Church discerned which writings are to be included in the list of the sacred books." (CCC 120)

- "Tobit, Judith...1 and 2 Maccabees...Wisdom, Sirach (Ecclesiasticus)...Baruch" (CCC 120)
- **READ THE APOCRYPHA FOR YOURSELF HERE:** www.biblestudytools.com/rhe/

Problematic passages of The Deuterocanon to Consider:

1. Fish Sacrifices To Drive Away The Demonic

- **Tobit 6:5-7** "Then the angel said to him: Take out the entrails of this fish, and lay up his heart, and his gall, and his liver for thee: for these are necessary for useful medicines. 6 And when he had done so, he roasted the flesh thereof, and they took it with them in the way: the rest they salted as much as might serve them, till they came to Rages the city of the Medes. 7 Then Tobias asked the angel, and said to him: I beseech thee, brother Azarias, tell me what remedies are these things good for, which thou hast bid me keep of the fish? 8 And the angel, answering, said to him: If thou put a little piece of its heart upon coals, **the smoke thereof driveth away all kind of devils, either from man or from woman, so that they come no more to them.**"
- **Tobit 6:19**"burn the the liver of yonder fish, and therewith the demon shall be driven away"
- **Tobit 8:2-3** "remembering what the angel had said, he took out from his wallet a piece of the fish's liver, which he burnt on live coals. With that, the evil spirit fled; it was overtaken by the angel Raphael in the waste lands of Upper Egypt, and there held prisoner"
- **Tobit 11:13-15** "Tobias took out the fish's gall and rubbed it on his father's eyes. He waited, maybe, for half an hour...and immediately his father's sight was restored."
- **This practice of burning the fish's guts to drive the demonic**

away is identical to witchcraft. Is there any biblical justification for it?

- Deuteronomy 18:9–14 "When you come into the land that the LORD your God is giving you, you shall not learn to follow the abominable practices of those nations. [10] There shall not be found among you anyone who burns his son or his daughter as an offering, anyone who practices divination or tells fortunes or interprets omens, or a sorcerer [11] or a charmer or a medium or a necromancer or one who inquires of the dead, [12] for whoever does these things is an abomination to the LORD. And because of these abominations the LORD your God is driving them out before you. [13] You shall be blameless before the LORD your God, [14] for these nations, which you are about to dispossess, listen to fortune-tellers and to diviners. But as for you, the LORD your God has not allowed you to do this." (ESV)
- Deuteronomy 32:17 "They sacrificed to demons that were no gods, to gods they had never known, to new gods that had come recently, whom your fathers had never dreaded." (ESV)
- 1 Corinthians 10:20 "No, I imply that what pagans sacrifice they offer to demons and not to God. I do not want you to be participants with demons." (ESV)

2. Giving Money For The Forgiveness Of Sin

- **Tobit 4:11** "For **alms deliver from all sin, and from death**, and will not suffer the soul to go into darkness."
- **Tobit 12:9** "For **alms delivereth from death**, and the same is that which **purgeth away sins**, and maketh to **find mercy and life everlasting**."
- **Sirach 3:3, 30** "Whoso honoureth his father maketh an atonement for his sins...Water will quench a flaming fire; and alms maketh an atonement for sin"
- The Bible speaks clearly about giving being willing and joyous, not out of motives of avoiding Hell by buying your forgiveness.

Scripture is clear that forgiveness comes through faith in Jesus alone.

- **Why does Sirach say honoring one's father makes an atonement for sins? Where is that in the Bible? Doesn't that oppose the clear teaching of Galatians 2:16 and many other passages which explain justification does not come by works, but by faith in Jesus Christ?**
  - Galatians 2:16 "yet we know that a person is not justified by works of the law but through faith in Jesus Christ, so we also have believed in Christ Jesus, in order to be justified by faith in Christ and not by works of the law, because by works of the law no one will be justified." (ESV)
- **Does giving make an "atonement for sin" or "purgeth away sins"? Isn't that contrary to 1 John 1:7 and Hebrews 9:14 & 22?**
  - 1 John 1:7 "the blood of Jesus his Son cleanses us from all sin" (ESV)
  - Hebrews 9:14 "how much more will the blood of Christ, who through the eternal Spirit offered himself without blemish to God, purify our conscience from dead works to serve the living God." (ESV)
  - Hebrews 9:22 "Indeed, under the law almost everything is purified with blood, and without the shedding of blood there is no forgiveness of sins." (ESV)

3. Overemphasis On Angels

- **Tobit 3:24** "Raphael, one of the Lord's holy angels, was sent out, bearing common deliverance to the suppliants of a single hour"
- **Tobit 12:15** "I am the angel Raphael, and my place is among those seven who stand in the presence of the Lord"
- **Tobit 12:15** "the angel Raphael, one of the seven, who stand before the Lord"

- Why is Raphael/Azarias not referenced or mentioned in the Protestant canon of the Bible? Why does Tobit have so many references (almost every chapter multiple times) to angels compared to other books of the Bible?
- Why are Michael and Gabriel the only named angels in the Protestant canon of the Bible? (Daniel 8:16, 21; 10:13,21; 12:1, Luke 1:9-26; Jude 1:9, Revelation 12:7)
- Why does the name Raphael appear for angels in Islam, Mormonism, the Babylonian Talmud, and the book of 1 Enoch?
- Tobit 12:16-22 "the fell down trembling, face to earth. Peace be with you, the angel said…for three hours together, face to earth, they gave thanks to God"
- When Tobias and his father fall down before the angel Raphael, why does the angel not stop them from bowing down (for three hours)? Like the angel rebukes John in Revelation 22:8-9 from bowing down in front of him?
- Revelation 22:8–9 "I, John, am the one who heard and saw these things. And when I heard and saw them, I fell down to worship at the feet of the angel who showed them to me, [9] but he said to me, "You must not do that! I am a fellow servant with you and your brothers the prophets, and with those who keep the words of this book. Worship God." (ESV)

4. Not Helping Sinners

Sirach 12:4-7 advices, "Give to the godly man, and help not a sinner. Do well unto him that is lowly, but give not to the ungodly; hold back thy bread, and give it not unto him… give unto the good, and help not the sinner."

Tobit 4:17 "Bestow thy meat and thy drink upon a just man's burying, never share them with sinners."

- Is this in line with Jesus' commands and other biblical guidance?

- Proverbs 25:21–22 "If your enemy is hungry, give him bread to eat, and if he is thirsty, give him water to drink, [22] for you will heap burning coals on his head, and the LORD will reward you." (ESV)
- Luke 6:27–31 "But I say to you who hear, Love your enemies, do good to those who hate you, [28] bless those who curse you, pray for those who abuse you. [29] To one who strikes you on the cheek, offer the other also, and from one who takes away your cloak do not withhold your tunic either. [30] Give to everyone who begs from you, and from one who takes away your goods do not demand them back. [31] And as you wish that others would do to you, do so to them." (ESV)
- Romans 12:20–21 "To the contrary, "if your enemy is hungry, feed him; if he is thirsty, give him something to drink; for by so doing you will heap burning coals on his head." [21] Do not be overcome by evil, but overcome evil with good." (ESV)

5. Born Good, Without Sin

- **Wisdom 8:19,20** " For I was a witty child, and had a good spirit. Yea rather, being good, I came into a body undefiled."
- Is anyone born without sin? Is anyone without sin? What does 1 John 1:8 say about that? How could the author of *Wisdom* be an exception?
- 1 John 1:8 "If we say we have no sin, we deceive ourselves, and the truth is not in us." (ESV)
- Romans 3:23 "for all have sinned and fall short of the glory of God" (ESV)
- Romans 3:10 "None is righteous, no, not one" (ESV)
- Romans 5:12 "Therefore, just as sin came into the world through one man, and death through sin, and so death spread to all men because all sinned"
- Romans 5:18–19 "Therefore, as one trespass led to condemnation for all men, so one act of righteousness leads to

justification and life for all men. [19] For as by the one man's disobedience the many were made sinners, so by the one man's obedience the many will be made righteous." (ESV)

- Psalm 51:5 "Behold, I was brought forth in iniquity, and in sin did my mother conceive me."
- Jeremiah 17: 9 "The heart is deceitful above all things, and desperately sick; who can understand it?"

6. Offerings And Prayers For The Dead

- **2 Maccabees 12:43** "And making a gathering, **he sent** twelve thousand drachms of **silver** to Jerusalem for sacrifice **to be offered for the sins of the dead**, thinking well and religiously concerning the resurrection."
- **2 Maccabees 12:44-46** "For if he had not hoped that the that were slain should rise again, it would have seemed superfluous and vain to **pray for the dead,** 45 And because he considered that the who had fallen asleep with godliness, **had great grace laid up for them.** 46 It is therefore a holy and wholesome thought to **pray for the dead, that they may be loosed from sins.**"
- **Is there anywhere in the Bible that supports the practice of offerings or prayers for the dead?**

7. Historical Errors

- **Judith 1:5** "Now in the twelfth year of his reign, Nabuchodon-osor, king of the Assyrians, who reigned in Ninive the great city, fought against Arphaxad and overcame him."
- **Why does Judith claim Nebuchadnezzar to be the king of the Assyrians when he was the king of the Babylonians?**
- "Nebuchadnezzar the king of Babylon" appears over 50 times in the Bible and even more across historical artifacts. He is

never referenced as a king of Assyria anywhere other than this passage. Why does this passage get it wrong?
- 2 Kings 24:1 "Nebuchadnezzar king of Babylon"

- **Baruch 6:2**, "And when you are come into Babylon, you shall be there many years, and for a long time, even to seven generations: and after that I will bring you away from thence with peace."
- **Jeremiah 25:11** says the Jews would serve in Babylon for **70 years while Baruch says seven generations. Why the difference?**
  - Jeremiah 25:11 "This whole land shall become a ruin and a waste, and these nations shall serve the king of Babylon seventy years." (ESV)
  - ESV Study Bible Note: "This is probably counted from the first exile in 605 B.C. to the first return, variously dated from 538 to 535 (2 Chron. 36:21; Ezra 1:1). However, 70 may be a rounded number, as it is elsewhere (Ps. 90:10; cf. Matt. 18:22)."

8. Other Concerning Passages

- Sirach (Ben Sira) 40:29-30 "My son, in thy lifetime be not indigent: for it is better to die than to want. 30 The life of him that looketh toward another man's table is not to be counted a life: for he feedeth his soul with another man's meat."
- [You should divorce if your wife does not obey you] Sirach 25:35-36 "If she walk not at thy hand, she will confound thee in the sight of thy enemies. 36 Cut her off from thy flesh, lest she always abuse thee."
- Jeremiah took the tabernacle of the ark to a cave in the mountain Moses saw Canaan. 2 Maccabees 2:1-16
- 2 Maccabees 2:5 "And when Jeremias came thither he found a hollow cave: and he carried in thither the tabernacle, and the ark, and the altar of incense, and so stopped the door."

- Wisdom 7:26 "For she is the brightness of eternal light, and the unspotted mirror of God's majesty, and the image of his goodness."
- Wisdom 9:19 "For by wisdom they were healed, whosoever have pleased thee, O Lord, from the beginning."
- " Sirach implies our actions can bring favor upon ourselves, mitigate our sin in God's eyes, and anticipate reciprocal responses from those we assist in their time of need" (chapters 3, 7, 12, 17, and 22)

Four Reasons the Apocrypha/ Deuterocanon Should Not Be in the Bible

By Dr. Wayne Grudem, from: www.biblicaltraining.org/library/ canon-scripture-wayne-grudem

(1) they do not claim for themselves the same kind of authority as the Old Testament writings;

(2) they were not regarded as God's words by the Jewish people from whom they originated;
- "When these lists are examined, we find that the earlier ones omit the Apocrypha, and that the later ones (beginning at the end of the fourth century in the West) include it. The Apocrypha began to be put on the same level as our canonical books at about the same time as many other innovations entered into the Church." www.bible-researcher.com/ canon1.html

(3) they were not considered to be Scripture by Jesus or the New Testament authors;
- "This fact is confirmed by the quotations of Jesus and

the New Testament authors from the Old Testament. According to one count, Jesus and the New Testament authors quote various parts of the Old Testament Scriptures as divinely authoritative over 295 times, but not once do they cite any statement from the books of the Apocrypha or any other writings as having divine authority." www.biblicaltraining.org/library/canon-scripture-wayne-grudem

- Some of the quotes in the NT of the OT: www.bible-researcher.com/quote01.html
- No book out of the Canon is quoted from except perhaps the word of Enoch in Jude. - "There are other Hebrew works that are mentioned in the Bible that God directed the authors to use. Some of these include the Book of the Wars of the Lord (Numbers 21:14), the Book of Samuel the Seer, the Book of Nathan the Prophet, and the Book of Gad the Seer (1 Chronicles 29:29). Also, there are the Acts of Rehoboam and the Chronicles of the Kings of Judah (1 Kings 14:29). We also know that Solomon composed more than a thousand songs (1 Kings 4:32), yet only two are preserved in the book of Psalms (72 and 127). Writing under the inspiration of the Holy Spirit in the New Testament, Paul included a quotation from the Cretan poet Epimenides (Titus 1:12) and quoted from the poets Epimenides and Aratus in his speech at Athens (Acts 17:28)." www.gotquestions.org/book-of-Jasher.html
- NOTE: The N.T. does not quote from Esther, Ecclesiastes, Song of Solomon or Obadiah either. www.biblequery.org/Bible/BibleCanon/WhatAboutTheApocrypha.html

(4) they contain teachings inconsistent with the rest of the Bible.

A Brief History of the
Canon of the Bible

- Peter recognized Paul's writings as Scripture (2 Peter 3:15-16) & Some of the books of the New Testament were being circulated among the churches (Colossians 4:16; 1 Thessalonians 5:27).
- In **90 AD.** the Jewish Council at Jamnia excluded from the Old Testament all but the writings Jews and Protestants accept today.
- by **A.D. 250** there was nearly universal agreement on the canon of Hebrew Scripture
- Paul considered Luke's writings to be as authoritative as the Old Testament (1 Timothy 5:18; see also Deuteronomy 25:4 and Luke 10:7)
- Clement of Rome mentioned at least eight New Testament books (**A.D. 95**).
- Polycarp, a disciple of John the apostle, acknowledged 15 books (**A.D. 108**).
- Ignatius of Antioch acknowledged about seven NT books (**A.D. 115**).
- Muratorian Canon - (**A.D. 180**) 22 of 27 NT books www.gotquestions.org/Muratorian-Canon.html
- Later, Irenaeus mentioned 21 books (**A.D. 185**) & Hippolytus recognized 22 books (**A.D. 170-235**).
- The NT books receiving the most controversy were Hebrews, James, 2 Peter, 2 John, and 3 John
- History of when the Books of the Bible were written: www.bible-researcher.com/history1.html
- The first "canon" was the Muratorian Canon, which was compiled in **AD 170**
- The Muratorian Canon included all of the New Testament books except Hebrews, James, 1 and 2 Peter, and 3 John - www.bible-researcher.com/muratorian.html

- In **AD 363**, the Council of Laodicea stated that only the Old Testament (along with one book of the Apocrypha) and 26 books of the New Testament (everything but Revelation) were canonical and to be read in the churches.
- **Jerome on the Canon - on omitting most of the Apocrypha due to it being in Greek and not Hebrew**: www.bible-researcher.com/jerome.html
- Hebrew Bible VS. Greek Septuagint VS. Latin Vulgate - www.bible-researcher.com/canon2.html
- "The first direct application of the term canon to the Scriptures seems to be in the verses of Amphilochius (**cir. 380 A.D.**), where the word indicates the rule by which the contents of the Bible must be determined, and thus secondarily an index of the constituent books."
- "Among Christians there was no consensus until Jerome died and **Augustine championed the Apocrypha at the Council of Carthage in 397 AD**. These writings were in Bibles used by Christians for over 1,100 years. Even the King James Bible originally included it."
- "The Council of Hippo (**AD 393**) & the Council of Carthage (**AD 397**) also affirmed the same 27 books as authoritative."
- "**Many early Christian leaders did not believe the Apocrypha scripture.** Some are: Athanasius, Ambrose, Amphilochus, Athanasius, Cyril of Jerusalem, Gregory Nanzianzus, Jerome, Melito of Sardis, and Origen. The Jews Josephus and Philo also rejected it. Many others, such as Justin Martyr, **wrote volumes yet never once cited it.** Athanasius and Ambrose were inconsistent. Even many for it, like Augustine, **believed it inspired in a lesser way.**"
- First Council of Nicaea (AD 325), First Council of Constantinople (AD 381), Council of Ephesus (AD 431), Council of Chalcedon (AD 451), Second Council of Constantinople (AD 553), Third Council of Constantinople (AD 680), and Second Council of Nicaea (AD 787)
- **1380-1382** John Wycliffe and associates make first translation of the whole Bible into English

- **1388** John Purvey revises Wycliffe Bible
- **1455 Gutenberg's** Latin Bible—first from press
- **1516** Erasmus's Greek New Testament, forerunner to the Textus Receptus used by KJV translators
- **1522** Martin Luther translated the New Testament into German (**complete Bible in 1534**)
- Roman Catholic Church officially added the Apocrypha / Deuterocanonicals to their Bible at the **Council of Trent in AD 1546**

Helpful Links for More Information

- **READ THE APOCRYPHA FOR YOURSELF HERE: www.biblestudytools.com/rhe/**

- **The Apocrypha/Deuterocanon** - www.gotquestions.org/apocrypha-deuterocanonical.html
- The books of the Apocrypha include 1 Esdras, 2 Esdras, Tobit, Judith, Wisdom of Solomon, Ecclesiasticus, Baruch, the Letter of Jeremiah, Prayer of Manasseh, 1 Maccabees, and 2 Maccabees, as well as additions to the books of Esther and Daniel. Not all of these books are included in Catholic Bibles. www.bible-researcher.com/canon2.html#reform

  - **1 & 2 Esdras** - www.gotquestions.org/first-second-Esdras.html

  - **The Book of Tobit** - www.gotquestions.org/book-of-Tobit.html

  - **Book of Judith** - www.gotquestions.org/book-of-Judith.html

  - **The Book of Enoch** - www.gotquestions.org/book-of-Enoch.html

  - **The Wisdom of Solomon** - www.gotquestions.org/Wisdom-of-Solomon.html

- **Ecclesiasticus (Sirach)** - www.gotquestions.org/book-of-Ecclesiasticus.html

- **Baruch** - www.gotquestions.org/book-of-Baruch.html

- **The Letter of Jeremiah** - www.gotquestions.org/letter-of-Jeremiah.html

- **The Prayer of Manasseh** - www.gotquestions.org/Prayer-of-Manasseh.html

- **1 & 2 Maccabees** - www.gotquestions.org/first-second-Maccabees.html
  - 2 Maccabees discusses several doctrinal issues, including prayers and sacrifices for the dead, intercession of the saints, and resurrection on Judgment Day. The Catholic Church has based the doctrines of purgatory and masses for the dead on this work.

- **Additions to Esther** - www.gotquestions.org/Book-Esther-God.html
  - Extra chapters - www.biblestudytools.com/rhe/additions-to-esther

- **Additions to Daniel** -
  - Bel and the Dragon - www.gotquestions.org/Bel-and-the-Dragon.html
  - Prayer of Azariah (addition to Daniel 3) - www.gotquestions.org/Prayer-of-Azariah.html
  - Book of Susana - www.gotquestions.org/book-of-Susanna.html
- www.gotquestions.org/content_Bible_apocrypha.html

BOTTOM LINE: Very few early church fathers quoted or referenced the Apocrypha/Deuterocanon with any consistency. It wasn't until after Constantine became Emperor and the Edict of Milan (313 A.D.) was issued that the Apocryphal books began to gain validity, primarily under Latin/Roman church leaders.

Here are Apocryphal books early Christian writers referred to:
(references below accessed from: www.biblequery.org/Bible/
BibleCanon/WhatAboutTheApocrypha.html)

Cr 1 Clement (of Rome) (16 pgs) 96/98 A.D.
Ba Epistle of Barnabas (13 pgs) c.100 A.D.
Ig Ignatius (21 pgs) c.110-117 A.D.
Pa Papias disciple of John (3 pgs) 110-113 A.D.
Di Didache (Teach. of 12 Disc.)(6 pgs) before 125 A.D.
Dg (anonymous) to Diognetus (6 pgs) c.130 A.D.
Po Polycarp, disciple of John (4 pgs) c.150 A.D.
Jm Justin Martyr (119 pgs) c.138-165 A.D.
He Shepherd of Hermas (47 pgs) 160 A.D.
Th Theophilus [Antioch] (33 pgs) 168-181/188 A.D.
Me Melito of Sardis (11 pgs) 170-177 A.D.
Ae Athenagoras (34 pgs) c.177 A.D.
Ir Irenaeus (264 pgs) 182-188 A.D.
Ca Clement of Alexan. (424 pgs) 193-217/220 A.D.
Te Tertullian [Rome] (854 pgs) 200-220 A.D.
Hi Hippolytus, (233 pgs) 225-235/6 A.D.
Or Origen (622 pgs) 230-254 A.D.
Nv Novatian (39 pgs) 250-257 A.D.
an Anonymous against Novatian(7 pgs) c.255 A.D.
And Treatise on Rebaptism (11 pgs)
Cp Cyprian and friends (270 pgs) 248-258 A.D.
Not shown are Bardesan (154-230) [ref. to Gen] or Julius Africanus (232-245
A.D.). [Neh,Dan by name, allude Ex]

W = Books or quotes mentioned by name or by writer
G = Mentioned as words of God + quoted
B = Mentioned as scripture or quoted + "it is written"
Q = quote of 1 or more verses. 1/2 = quote of 1/2 a verse
A = Allusion. - = no reference

Writer	Cr	Ba	Ig	Pa	Di	Dg	Po	JM	He	Th	Me	Ae	Ir	Ca	Te	Hi	Or	JA	Nv	an	Cp
Tobit	·	·	·	·	·	·	1/2	·	·	·	X	·	·	W	·	A	W	·	·	·	W
Judith	W	·	·	·	·	·	·	·	·	·	X	·	·	W	·	·	A	·	·	·	
Wisdom	W	·	·	·	·	·	·	·	·	·	X	·	·	Q	·	·	·	·	·	·	W
Ecclus	·	·	·	·	·	·	·	·	·	·	X	·	·	·	·	·	·	·	·	Q	W
Baruch	·	·	·	·	·	·	·	·	·	·	X	·	·	Q	·	Q	·	·	·	·	W
Bel	·	·	·	·	·	·	·	·	·	·	X	·	·	·	A	·	W	·	·	·	A
Susan	·	·	·	·	·	·	·	·	·	·	X	·	W	W	W	W	W	X	·	·	W
3 Holy	·	·	·	·	·	·	·	·	·	·	X	·	·	·	·	A	·	·	·	·	W
Manass	·	·	·	·	·	·	·	·	·	·	X	·	·	·	·	·	·	·	·	·	
3 Esdra	·	·	·	·	·	·	·	·	·	·	X	·	·	·	·	·	Q	·	·	·	
Esdras - general	·	·	·	·	·	·	·	W	·	·	W	·	·	·	·	·	·	·	·	·	W
1,2 Mac	·	·	·	·	·	·	·	·	·	·	X	·	·	1/2 W	·	·	W	·	·	·	W
3,4 Mac	·	·	·	·	·	·	·	·	·	·	X	·	·	·	·	·	·	·	·	·	
Writer	Cr	Ba	Ig	Pa	Di	Dg	Po	JM	He	Th	Me	Ae	Ir	Ca	Te	Hi	Or	JA	Nv	an	Cp
Time	96/98 A.D.							150 A.D.		168 A.D.				200			225 A.D. 258 A.D.				
Pages	151 pages							135 pgs						284	854	424	225	622	8	57 pgs	270

Melito of Sardis excluded, Nehemiah, Esther, and the Apocrypha according to
http://www.earlychurch.org.uk/melito.php.

Disputed Books of the OldTestament

The table below shows which of the disputed Old Testament books are included in Christian catalogs of canonical books up to the eighth century.

Y indicates that the book is plainly listed as Holy Scripture;

N indicates that it is placed in an inferior class of books;

M indicates that the terminology of the author may be construed as a reference to the book as Holy Scripture.

An S indicates that the author does not mention the book in his catalog, which implies its rejection.

See notes on the authorities below.
http://www.bible-researcher.com/canon4.html

Esth. - Esther
Bar. - Baruch
Eccl. - Ecclesiasticus
Wisd. - Wisdom of Solomon
Tob. - Tobit
Jud. - Judith
Mac. - First and Second Maccabees

1. Greek Authors.	Date	Esth.	Bar.	Eccl.	Wisd.	Tob.	Jud.	Mac.
Melito	160	S	S	S	S	S	S	S
Origen	225	Y	M	S	S	S	S	N
Cyril of Jerusalem	348	Y	Y	N	N	N	N	N
Council of Laodicea	363	Y	Y	S	S	S	S	S
Athanasius	367	N	Y	N	N	N	N	S
Gregory of Nazianzus	380	S	S	S	S	S	S	S
Amphilocius of Iconium	380	M	S	S	S	S	S	S
Epiphanius	385	Y	S	N	N	S	S	S
Stichometry of Niceph.	550	N	Y	N	N	N	N	N
Synopsis of Sac. Scrip.	550	N	S	N	N	N	N	N
Leontius	590	S	S	S	S	S	S	S
List of the Sixty Books	650	N	S	N	N	N	N	N
John of Damascus	730	Y	S	N	N	S	S	S
2. Syrian Greek.	Date	Esth.	Bar.	Eccl.	Wisd.	Tob.	Jud.	Mac.
"Apostolic Canons"	380	Y	S	N	S	S	M	Y
3. Latin Authors.*	Date	Esth.	Bar.	Eccl.	Wisd.	Tob.	Jud.	Mac.
Hilary of Poitiers	360	Y	M	S	S	M	M	S
Cheltenham List	360	Y	M	S	M	Y	Y	Y
Jerome	390	Y	M	N	N	N	N	N
Augustine	397	Y	M	Y	Y	Y	Y	Y
3rd Council of Carthage	397	Y	M	Y	Y	Y	Y	Y
Rufinus	400	Y	M	N	N	N	N	N
Codex Claromontanus	400	Y	M	Y	Y	Y	Y	Y
Letter of Innocent I	405	Y	M	Y	Y	Y	Y	Y
Decree of Gelasius	550	Y	Y	Y	Y	Y	Y	Y
Cassiodorus	560	Y	M	Y	Y	Y	Y	Y
Isidore of Seville	625	Y	M	Y	Y	Y	Y	Y

A few notes on the **Pseudepigrapha:** (available at: www.gotquestions.org/pseudepigrapha.html)

1) they were written under **false names**

2) They contain anachronisms and historical errors

3) They contain outright heresy
   - Examples: Testament of Hezekiah, the Vision of Isaiah, the Books of Enoch, the Secrets of Enoch, the Book of Noah, the Apocalypse of Baruch (Baruch was Jeremiah's scribe according to Jeremiah 36:4), the Rest of the Words of Baruch, the Psalter of Solomon, the Odes of Solomon, the Testaments of the Twelve Patriarchs, the Testament of Adam, the Testament of Abraham, the Testament of Job, the Apocalypse of Ezra, the Prayer of Joseph, Elijah the Prophet, Zechariah the Prophet, Zechariah: Father of John, the Itinerary of Paul, the Acts of Paul, the Apocalypse of Paul, the Itinerary of Peter, the Itinerary of Thomas, the Gospel According to Thomas, the History of James, the Apocalypse of Peter, and the Epistles of Barnabas.

HELPFUL AND IMPORTANT SCRIPTURES

What are the "Five Solas"

The "five solas" describe a summary of some of the major concerns and focuses of those who sought reform in the church in the 1500s during the "Protestant Reformation." "Sola" means alone and was used to define the essential elements of the Christian faith. The "reformers" of the day saw many things being added to the pure teachings of the Bible. Their corrective focus was found in their theological convictions about: 1) Scripture, 2) Faith, 3) Grace, 4) Christ, & 5) God's Glory
when understanding God's plans for salvation in the Gospel.

Here Are Some Verses I Think Are Helpful In Explaining Each Of These Areas:

SCRIPTURE ALONE

The Bible alone is our greatest authority.
The What (Authoritative Communication) of Our Salvation

<u>Scripture over Tradition and the Magisterium.</u>
This does not mean that truth is not found elsewhere.
It means that all we learn about God, His Creation,
and His plan for life and eternity should be inter-
preted in view of the Scriptures. The Bible is sufficient for our theological understanding.

The Bible Is From God

- 2 Peter 1:19-21 "And we have the prophetic word more *fully confirmed*, to which you will do well to *pay attention* as to a lamp shining in a dark place, until the day dawns and the morning star rises in your hearts, [20] knowing this first of all, that no prophecy of Scripture comes from someone's own interpretation. [21] For no prophecy was ever produced by the will of man, but *men spoke from God* as they were carried along by the Holy Spirit." (ESV)
- 2 Timothy 3:16-17 "All Scripture is *breathed out by God* and profitable for teaching, for reproof, for correction, and for training in righteousness, that the man of God *may be complete*, equipped for every good work."
- Jesus in John 5:39-40 "the Scriptures...bear witness about me"
- James 1:17 "Every good gift and every perfect gift is from above, coming down *from the Father* of lights with whom there is no variation or shadow due to change."
- Deuteronomy 18:20 "But the prophet who presumes to speak a word in my name that I have not commanded him to speak, or who speaks in the name of other gods, that same prophet shall die.'"

The Bible Is Sufficient For Salvation

- 2 Peter 1:3 "His divine power has *granted to us all things that pertain to life and godliness*, through the knowledge of him who

called us to his own glory and excellence" (ESV)
- 2 Timothy 3:10-17 "the sacred writings, which are able to make you wise for salvation through faith in Christ Jesus."
- James 1:21 "receive with meekness the implanted word, which is able to save your souls"
- Ephesians 6:17 "take...the sword of the Spirit, which is the word of God" Ephesians 6:17
- Psalm 119:105 "Your word is a lamp to my feet and a light to my path."
- Mark 12:24 "Jesus said to them, 'Is this not the reason you are wrong, because you know neither the Scriptures nor the power of God?'"
- Joshua 1:7-8 "This Book of the Law shall not depart from your mouth, but you shall meditate on it day and night, so that you may be careful to do according to all that is written in it. For then you will make your way prosperous, and then you will have good success."
- Jude 3 "Beloved, although I was very eager to write to you about our common salvation, I found it necessary to write appealing to you to contend for the faith that was *once for all delivered to the saints.*"
- John 20:30-31 "Now Jesus did many other signs in the presence of the disciples, which are not written in this book; [31] but *these are written so that you may believe that Jesus is the Christ, the Son of God, and that by believing you may have life in his name.*"

Do Not Add Or Take Away From The Bible's Teaching & Authority

- Deuteronomy 4:2 "*You shall not add* to the word that I command you, nor take from it, that you may keep the commandments of the LORD your God that I command you." (ESV)
- Deuteronomy 12:32 "Everything that I command you, you shall be careful to do. *You shall not add to it or take from it.*"

- Ecclesiastes 3:14 "I perceived that whatever God does *endures forever; nothing can be added to it, nor anything taken from it.* God has done it, so that people fear before him."
- Proverbs 30:5–6 "Every word of God proves true; he is a shield to those who take refuge in him. [6] *Do not add to his words*, lest he rebuke you and you be found a liar."
- 2 John 9 "Everyone who goes on ahead and does not abide in the teaching of Christ, does not have God. Whoever *abides in the teaching* has both the Father and the Son."
- 1 Corinthians 4:6–7 "I have applied all these things to myself and Apollos for your benefit, brothers, that you may *learn by us not to go beyond what is written,* that none of you may be puffed up in favor of one against another. [7] For who sees anything different in you? What do you have that you did not receive? If then you received it, why do you boast as if you did not receive it?"
- 2 Timothy 2:15 "rightly handling the word of truth"
- Galatians 1:6–9 "I am astonished that you are so quickly deserting him who called you in the grace of Christ and are turning to a different gospel—[7] not that there is another one, but there are some who trouble you and want to distort the gospel of Christ. [8] But even if we or an angel from heaven should preach to you a gospel contrary to the one we preached to you, let him be accursed. [9] As we have said before, so now I say again: If anyone is preaching to you a gospel contrary to the one you received, let him be accursed."
- Revelation 22:18–19 "I warn everyone who hears the words of the prophecy of this book: if anyone adds to them, God will add to him the plagues described in this book, [19] and if anyone takes away from the words of the book of this prophecy, God will take away his share in the tree of life and in the holy city, which are described in this book."

Relevant Warnings - Do Not Turn
Away From The Bible

- 2 Timothy 4:3–4 "For the time is coming when people will not endure sound teaching, but having itching ears they will accumulate for themselves teachers to suit their own passions, [4] and will turn away from listening to the truth and wander off into myths." (ESV)
- 2 Peter 2:1 "But false prophets also arose among the people, just as there will be false teachers among you, who will secretly bring in destructive heresies"
- Jude 4 "For certain people have crept in unnoticed who long ago were designated for this condemnation, ungodly people, who pervert the grace of our God"
- Matthew 23:4 "They tie up heavy burdens, hard to bear, and lay them on people's shoulders"

FAITH ALONE

Salvation is received through faith alone in Jesus.

The How (Reception) of Our Salvation

Saved through Faith, not through Works, Church, Mass, or Sacraments

Jesus' finished work on the Cross and resurrection from the grave is our means of salvation. When we repent and believe (faith), we receive that free gift (grace) of salvation. Our trust in and treasuring of Jesus for forgiveness of sins and for eternal life with God we are saved. Our good works, religious obedience, church involvement, and sacraments do not cause, precede, or maintain our salvation. Good works are necessarily present in the lives of true believers as evidence and demonstration of saving faith.

- Galatians 1:9 "As we have said before, so now I say again: If anyone is preaching to you a gospel contrary to the one you received, let him be accursed." (ESV)
- Galatians 2:16 "yet we know that a person is not justified by works of the law but through faith in Jesus Christ, so we also have believed in Christ Jesus, in order to be justified by faith in Christ and not by works of the law, because by works of the law no one will be justified."
- Ephesians 2:8–9 "For by grace you have been saved through faith. And this is not your own doing; it is the gift of God, [9] not a result of works, so that no one may boast."
- NOTE FROM the *ESV Study Bible*: The verb form for "have been saved" (Gk. sesōsmenoi, perfect tense) communicates that the Christian's salvation is fully secured.
- James 2:17–18 "So also faith by itself, if it does not have works, is dead. [18] But someone will say, 'You have faith and I have works.' Show me your faith apart from your works, and I will show you my faith by my works."
- James 2:24 "You see that a person is justified by works and not by faith alone."
- Romans 3:24–27 "justified by his grace as a gift, through the redemption that is in Christ Jesus, [25] whom God put forward as a propitiation by his blood, to be received by faith. This was to show God's righteousness, because in his divine forbearance he had passed over former sins. [26] It was to show his righteousness at the present time, so that he might be just and the justifier of the one who has faith in Jesus. [27] Then what becomes of our boasting? It is excluded. By what kind of law? By a law of works? No, but by the law of faith."
- Romans 3:28 "For we hold that one is justified by faith apart

from works of the law."

- NOTE: "Paul is using the word justified to mean "declared righteous by God." Paul is speaking of God's legal declaration of us as righteous as Christ's righteousness is applied to our account. James is using the word justified to mean "being demonstrated and proved." www.gotquestions.org/faith-alone.html
- Ephesians 2:10 " For we are his workmanship, created in Christ Jesus for good works, which God prepared beforehand, that we should walk in them." (ESV)
- John 3:16 "For God so loved the world, that he gave his only Son, that whoever believes in him should not perish but have eternal life." (ESV)
- Romans 4:4–5 "Now to the one who works, his wages are not counted as a gift but as his due. [5] And to the one who does not work but believes in him who justifies the ungodly, his faith is counted as righteousness" (ESV)
- Romans 5:19 "For as by the one man's disobedience the many were made sinners, so by the one man's obedience the many will be made righteous" (ESV)

GRACE ALONE

We are saved by the Grace of God alone.

The What (Cause) of Our Salvation

Saved by God's grace, not by human merit.

Salvation is achieved by God's finished work (what He has done) on the cross, not by our goodness (what we do). Only Jesus has fulfilled the law and paid the sufficient sacrifice for the forgiveness of sin. He shows us mercy by becoming the propitiation for our sins, taking on the wrath of God, and becoming sin for our sake. His grace imputes His righteousness into true believers. The grace of God cannot be earned, merited, or achieved through obedience or sacraments.

- Galatians 3:10–11 "For all who rely on works of the law are under a curse; for it is written, 'Cursed be everyone who does not abide by all things written in the Book of the Law, and do them.' Now it is evident that no one is justified before God by the law, for 'The righteous shall live by faith.'" (ESV)
- Ephesians 2:4–6 "But God, being rich in mercy, because of the great love with which he loved us, [5] even when we were dead in our trespasses, made us alive together with Christ—by grace you have been saved—[6] and raised us up with him and seated us with him in the heavenly places in Christ Jesus"
- Ephesians 2:8–9 "For by grace you have been saved through faith. And this is not your own doing; it is the gift of God, [9] not a result of works, so that no one may boast."
  - NOTE FROM the *ESV Study Bible*: The verb form for "have been saved" (Gk. sesōsmenoi, perfect tense) communicates that the Christian's salvation is fully secured.
- Romans 3:24–25 "and are justified by his grace as a gift, through the redemption that is in Christ Jesus, [25] whom God put forward as a propitiation by his blood, to be received by faith. This was to show God's righteousness, because in his divine forbearance he had passed over former sins."
- Romans 5:8 "God shows his love for us in that while we were still sinners, Christ died for us."
- Romans 5:15–17 "But the free gift is not like the trespass. For if many died through one man's trespass, much more have the grace of God and the free gift by the grace of that one man Jesus Christ abounded for many. ...those who receive the abundance of grace and the free gift of righteousness reign in life through the one man Jesus Christ."

- Romans 6:15 "What then? Are we to sin because we are not under law but under grace? By no means!"
- Romans 6:23 "For the wages of sin is death, but the free gift of God is eternal life in Christ Jesus our Lord."
- In response to claims for the Mosaic Law and Tradition to be kept by the Gentiles for salvation (specifically here is the ceremonial law of circumcision) - Peter in Acts 15:8–11 "And God, who knows the heart, bore witness to them, by giving them the Holy Spirit just as he did to us, [9] and he made no distinction between us and them, having cleansed their hearts by faith. [10] Now, therefore, why are you putting God to the test by placing a yoke on the neck of the disciples that neither our fathers nor we have been able to bear? [11] But we believe that we will be saved through the grace of the Lord Jesus, just as they will."
- 1 John 2:4–6 "whoever says he abides in him ought to walk in the same way in which he walked."
- 2 Corinthians 5:21 "For our sake he made him to be sin who knew no sin, so that in him we might become the righteousness of God."

CHRIST ALONE

We are saved by Jesus Christ alone.

The Who (Cause) of Our Salvation

<u>Saved by Jesus, not through a church, religious leaders, or religious rituals.</u>

God reveals Himself sufficiently to us through His Son Jesus. God provides salvation and forgiveness through Jesus alone, not through human priests or spiritual leaders. We do not rely on a church, priests, or sacraments to know God not to experience the joy of His salvation. Jesus is our perfect high priest who is the only way to His Father in Heaven. Salvation is only found in the name of Jesus and no other human name or church name is necessary for forgiveness.

- John 1:14 "And the Word became flesh and dwelt among us, and we have seen his glory, glory as of the only Son from the Father, full of grace and truth." (ESV)
- John 1:17–18 "For the law was given through Moses; grace and truth came through Jesus Christ. [18] No one has ever seen God; the only God, who is at the Father's side, he has made him known."
- John 14:6 "Jesus said to him, "I am the way, and the truth, and the life. No one comes to the Father except through me."
- Acts 4:12 "And there is salvation in no one else, for there is no other name under heaven given among men by which we must be saved."
- Romans 10:9–10 "because, if you confess with your mouth that Jesus is Lord and believe in your heart that God raised him from the dead, you will be saved. [10] For with the heart one believes and is justified, and with the mouth one confesses and is saved."
- Romans 10:13–15 "For 'everyone who calls on the name of the Lord will be saved.' [14] How then will they call on him in whom they have not believed? And how are they to believe in him of whom they have never heard? And how are they to hear without someone preaching? [15] And how are they to preach unless they are sent? As it is written, "How beautiful are the feet of those who preach the good news!"
- 2 John 9 "Everyone who goes on ahead and does not abide in the teaching of Christ, does not have God. Whoever abides in the teaching has both the Father and the Son."
- Revelation 19:16 "On his robe and on his thigh he has a name written, King of kings and Lord of lords"
- Hebrews 4:14 "Since then we have a great high priest who has

passed through the heavens, Jesus, the Son of God, let us hold fast our confession."
- Galatians 3:13 "Christ redeemed us from the curse of the law by becoming a curse for us"
- 1 Timothy 2:5 "For there is one God, and there is one mediator between God and men, the man Christ Jesus"
- Revelation 5:9–10 "And they sang a new song, saying, 'Worthy are you to take the scroll and to open its seals, for you were slain, and by your blood you ransomed people for God from every tribe and language and people and nation, [10] and you have made them a kingdom and priests to our God, and they shall reign on the earth."
- Colossians 1:18 "And he is the head of the body, the church. He is the beginning, the firstborn from the dead, that in every-thing he might be preeminent."

GOD'S GLORY ALONE
We exist to enjoy and honor our Creator.

The Why (Purpose) of Our Salvation and Life

<u>Purposed for God, by God, in God.</u>

God's primary motive in salvation is to display His love, goodness, and glory. The Bible and Creation is not centralized about humanity; their focus is on displaying and communicating the reality and char-acter of God. Humanity's goal in life should not be to improve their lives, elevate their image, or achieve their ambitions and pleasures. The purpose of our salvation and life is to enjoy Jesus and to point humanity to Him alone.

- 2 Peter 1:3 "His divine power has granted to us all things that pertain to life and godliness, through the knowledge of him who called us to his own glory and excellence" (ESV)
- Isaiah 6:3 - And one called to another and said: "Holy, holy, holy is the LORD of hosts; the whole earth is full of his glory!"
- Isaiah 48:11 - "For my own sake, for my own sake, I do it … My glory I will not give to another."
- John 5:44 "How can you believe, when you receive glory from one another and do not seek the glory that comes from the only God?"
- 2 Corinthians 3:18 "And we all, with unveiled face, beholding the glory of the Lord, are being transformed into the same image from one degree of glory to another. For this comes from the Lord who is the Spirit."
- 1 Corinthians 1:30-31 "And because of him you are in Christ Jesus, who became to us wisdom from God, righteousness and sanctification and redemption, so that, as it is written, 'Let the one who boasts, boast in the Lord.'"
- 1 Corinthians 3:19–23 "For the wisdom of this world is folly with God. For it is written, "He catches the wise in their craftiness," [20] and again, "The Lord knows the thoughts of the wise, that they are futile." [21] So let no one boast in men. For all things are yours, [22] whether Paul or Apollos or Cephas or the world or life or death or the present or the future—all are yours, [23] and you are Christ's, and Christ is God's."
- 1 Corinthians 3:4–9 "For when one says, "I follow Paul," and another, "I follow Apollos," are you not being merely human? What then is Apollos? What is Paul? Servants through whom you believed, as the Lord assigned to each. [6] I planted, Apollos watered, but God gave the growth. [7] So neither he who plants nor he who waters is anything, but only God who gives the growth. [8] He who plants and he who waters are one, and each will receive his wages according to his labor. [9] For we are God's fellow workers. You are God's field, God's building."

- Ephesians 2:8–9 "For by grace you have been saved through faith. And this is not your own doing; it is the gift of God, [9] not a result of works, so that no one may boast."
  - NOTE FROM the *ESV Study Bible*: The verb form for "have been saved" (Gk. sesōsmenoi, perfect tense) communicates that the Christian's salvation is fully secured.
- 1 Corinthians 10:31 "So, whether you eat or drink, or whatever you do, do all to the glory of God"
- John 15:5 "I am the vine; you are the branches. Whoever abides in me and I in him, he it is that bears much fruit, for apart from me you can do nothing."
- Galatians 3:2–3 "Let me ask you only this: Did you receive the Spirit by works of the law or by hearing with faith? [3] Are you so foolish? Having begun by the Spirit, are you now being perfected by the flesh?"
- James 1:17 "Every good gift and every perfect gift is from above, coming down from the Father of lights, with whom there is no variation or shadow due to change."
- Colossians 3:17 "And whatever you do, in word or deed, do everything in the name of the Lord Jesus, giving thanks to God the Father through him."

WHAT DOES THE BIBLE SAY ABOUT FALSE TEACHERS?

Ephesians 4:11-14 "that we may **no longer be children, tossed** to and fro by the waves and **carried** about by every wind of doctrine, **by human cunning**, by craftiness in deceitful schemes." (ESV)

Colossians 2:8 "**See to it that no one takes you captive by philosophy and empty deceit, according to human tradition**, according to the elemental spirits of the world, and not according to Christ."

What is a prophet? How can I recognize a true prophet from a false prophet? A prophet is a messenger of God who carries a message directly and personally related and is held to 100% consistency with Scripture and 100% fulfillment of any predictive statements. (Deuteronomy 13:1-5, 18: 15-22)

What is the difference between a prophet and a teacher? Both roles include the element of teaching, but a prophet claims a direct encounter with God (dream, vision, meeting, voice, event, etc.) where God revealed or spoke a particular message to him.

How can I recognize a true teacher from a bad teacher? A bad teacher from a false teacher? A bad teacher may misunderstand issues in Scripture or just do a poor job at instructing and exhorting people. A false teacher teaches "a different doctrine and does not agree with the sound words of our Lord

Jesus Christ" (1 Timothy 6:3) and goes against "sound doctrines" (Titus 1:9) specifically with an understanding towards who God is, what salvation is, and what the Scriptures say.

Isn't it wrong to publicly call out preachers, teachers, Christians, etc.? The issue of "opinions" between Christian brothers is different from the issue of "false teachings." Paul warns "not to quarrel over opinions" (v.1) in Romans 14, pointing out the dangers of "passing judgment" on a brother in Christ and how it can "destroy the work of God" (v.20). However, God commands us to "judge" those inside the church when their lifestyles (1 Corinthians 5:9-13) do not line up with God's Word. God also commands us to watch out for and confront false teachers who "teach a different doctrine and does not agree with the sound words of our Lord Jesus Christ." (1 Timothy 6:3). Pastors are specifically tasked to 1) "give instruction in sound doctrine" and 2) "rebuke those who contradict it" (Titus 1:9).

Should a false teacher be called out by name? If so, when? When a specific false teaching or teacher is affecting a body of believers (i.e. family, small group, church, denomination, region, nation), that false teaching and teacher must be named and confronted. Paul does this with both false teachings (1 Timothy 1:3-20 ; 6:2-10, Jude 1, 2 Peter 2, & many more) and with particular names (Alexander, Hymenaeus, & Philetus in 1 Timothy 1:20 and 2 Timothy 2:17).

What are some examples of false teachings? What are some characteristics of false teachers? There are many examples of false teachers with common descriptions (Galatians, 2 Peter, 1 & 2 Timothy, 1 & 2 John, Jude) that they may look and sound like Christians but that their teachings and lifestyle are not consistent with Scripture.

How can you call them false teachers when some of these people have doctrinal statements on their website and do many good things in getting the Bible and gospel into the hands of so many? Christianity is not a salvation of works and although some "good fruits" may seem exist in these ministries, they only mask the lies. The ends of a ministry (salvations, missions, good works) do not justify the means (a false gospel).

When false teachers lead people to Christ, are these converts

false believers? Not necessarily. If these believers have under-stood the gospel falsely, then their trust and faith in Jesus may be out of a greater love of Jesus' gifts rather than Jesus. Even if they have become true followers of Jesus, they need to study the Word of God, test their teachers, and be extremely cautious be-fore recommending a teacher to someone else.

Is it possible for false teachers to turn to truth and become true teachers? Yes, until we die, it is possible for anyone who is separated from God to turn to Him in salvation. Pray for their repentance and turning to the true Gospel of Christ.

If I have been following a false teacher, should I be embar-rassed or ashamed? What does God want me to do in response to realizing that I was following a false teacher? If you find that you have been following a bad or false teacher, repent of believing the lies that you heard/read and put on God's truths. If you have led or encouraged others towards those teachings/ teachers, guide them into the truth.

I still don't believe _____ is a false prophet/teacher, so how does this message matter for me? What should I do next? If you haven't been convinced from this outline, you need to be very concerned about your understanding of God, the Gospel, and His truths. Invest some time in reading the Scriptures to make sure you understand the teachings of God and not be misled by the traditions of men. Even if you haven't become convinced that he teachings of the Catechism of the Catholic Church is false, you need to begin to listen very closely to what you hear and read in the future. You need to make sure that who you listen to is trustworthy and is teaching the whole counsel of God accurately.

Matthew 15:1–9 "Then Pharisees and scribes came to Jesus from Jerusalem and said, [2] "Why do your disciples **break the tradition of the elders**? For they do not wash their hands when they eat." [3] He answered them, "**And why do you break the commandment of God for the sake of your tradition?** [4] For God commanded, 'Honor your father and your mother,' and, 'Whoever reviles father or mother must surely die.' [5] But you say, 'If anyone tells his father or his mother, "What you would have gained from me is given to God," [6] he need not honor his father.' So **for the sake of your tradition you have made void the word of God**. [7] You hypocrites! Well did Isaiah prophesy of you, when he said: [8] **"'This people honors me with their lips, but their heart is far from me; [9] in vain do they worship me, teaching as doctrines the commandments of men.'"** (ESV)

Mark 7:1–13 "in vain do they worship me, teaching as doctrines the commandments of men.' [8] You leave the commandment of God and hold to the tradition of men." [9] And he said to them, "You have a fine way of **rejecting the commandment of God in order to establish your tradition!** ... [13] **thus making void the word of God by your tradition that you have handed down. And many such things you do.**"

Galatians 1:13–16 "For you have heard of my former life in Judaism, how I persecuted the church of God violently and tried to destroy it. [14] And I was advancing in Judaism beyond many of my own age among my people, **so extremely zealous was I for the traditions** of my fathers."

False Teachers: Watch Out!
(2 Peter 2, ESV)

It is important to "triage" issues to understand the significance of beliefs. Here are three levels to use for categorizing various beliefs.

Believers Mature At Different Paces
3rd Level Issues: Allowable Individual Differences "As for the one who is weak in faith, welcome him, but not to quarrel over opinions. ...So then each of us will give an account to God." (Romans 14:1-12)

Less Faithful Teachers: Believing Christians, in Error
2nd Level Issues: Denominational Differences "Not many of

you should become teachers, my brothers, for you know that we who teach will be judged with greater strictness." (James 3:1)

False Teachers Misrepresent God & the Gospel
1st Level Issues: Christian vs. Non-Christian: Essential Teachings "built on the foundation of the apostles and prophets, Christ Jesus himself being the cornerstone" (Ephesians 2:20)
• *Who is God? What is the Gospel? What are the Scriptures?*

Here are some important truths from 2 Peter 2 about false teachers.

> 1. **PREPARE**! Their Presence is Guaranteed but is not Obvious to All – v.1

> 2. **WATCH**! False Teachers Are Characterized by:
False Words – v.3 ; Speaking Ignorantly – v.12 ; Endorse Sin – v.2, 13-15, 18 ; Greedy v.3, 14 ; Proud w/no accountability – v.10, 18 (Jude 8) ; Make Empty Promises – v.19 ; Rely on Experience/ Dreams (Jude 8) ; Speak Flippantly To Satan/Demons (2 Pet 2:10-13; Jude 8-10); Have Some Scriptural Knowledge, But Wander from It – v.20-22

"There are some things in them that are hard to understand, which the ignorant and unstable twist to their own destruction, as they do the other Scriptures." - 2 Peter 3:16

> 3. **CORRECT & WARN** Beloved, although I was very eager to write to you about our common salvation, I found it necessary to write appealing to you to contend for the faith that was once for all delivered to the saints. (Jude 1:3)
> · **Their Teachings Are Dangerous – v.1-3 – "destructive heresies"**
> · **False Teachings Are Characterized by: (Example, Pergamum, Revelation 2:12-17)**
Positive Thinking (self-focused prayers, name it/claim it, declarations)

Partial Truths (highlight the "positive"/easy, ignore the "negative"/difficult)

Promises (worship the gifts, not the giver)

Health, Wealth, & Prosperity (worldly-focused: good things into god things)

Legalism (works based salvation, self-righteousness)

License (freedom to sin) "pervert the grace of our God into sensuality" (Jude 1:4)

False Religions "deny our only Master and Lord, Jesus Christ" (Jude 1:4)

· **Their Punishment Is Guaranteed – v.1-10 (Jude)**

The Lord Knows How to Rescue the Righteous

(v.7-9) The Righteous Are… "distressed by the sensual conduct of the wicked"…"as that righteous man [Lot] lived among them day after day, he was tormenting his righteous soul over their lawless deeds that he saw and heard"

HOW CAN I BECOME A CHRISTIAN?

www.catholic.blog/christian

1. Understand and believe that God is the Creator of the Universe

God created us and has authority over us.

- Colossians 1:16-17 "For by him all things were created, in heaven and on earth, visible and invisible, whether thrones or dominions or rulers or authorities-all things were created through him and for him. 17 And he is before all things, and in him all things hold together."
- Hebrews 11:3 "By faith we understand that the universe was created by the word of God, so that what is seen was not made out of things that are visible."

We will give an answer for our lives.

- Hebrews 9:27 "And just as it is appointed for man to die once, and after that comes judgment"
- Hebrews 4:13 "And no creature is hidden from his sight, but all are naked and exposed to the eyes of him to whom we must give account."

2. Acknowledge and confess your sinfulness

God's Commandments are His perfect standard of Holiness.

- Romans 3:19-20 "Now we know that whatever the law says it speaks to those who are under the law, so that every mouth may be stopped, and the whole world may be held accountable to God. 20 For by works of the law no human being will be justified in his sight, since through the law comes knowledge of sin."
- Romans 3:23 "for all have sinned and fall short of the glory of God"
- James 2:10 "For whoever keeps the whole law but fails in one point has become accountable for all of it."

Admit that you are not good. Turn away from you sin and turn towards Christ.

- Psalm 32:5 "I acknowledged my sin to you, and I did not cover my iniquity; I said, 'I will confess my transgressions to the LORD,' and you forgave the iniquity of my sin."
- Romans 3:10-12 "None is righteous, no, not one; [11] no one understands; no one seeks for God. [12] All have turned aside; together they have become worthless; no one does good, not even one."
- 1 John 1:9-10 "If we confess our sins, he is faithful and just to forgive us our sins and to cleanse us from all unrighteousness. [10] If we say we have not sinned, we make him a liar, and his word is not in us."

3. Believe That Jesus Died On The Cross And Rose From The Grave

Realize that Salvation is by Faith (trusting in Jesus, loving and valuing Him more than anyone or anything) ***and not by good works.***

- Romans 6:23 "For the wages of sin is death, but the free gift of God is eternal life in Christ Jesus our Lord."

- Ephesians 2:8-9 "For by grace you have been saved through faith. And this is not your own doing; it is the gift of God, 9 not a result of works, so that no one may boast."

- Mark 12:28-31 "And one of the scribes came up and heard them disputing with one another, and seeing that he answered them well, asked him, 'Which commandment is the most important of all?' [29] Jesus answered, "The most important is, 'Hear, O Israel: The Lord our God, the Lord is one. [30] And you shall love the Lord your God with all your heart and with all your soul and with all your mind and with all your strength.' [31] The second is this: 'You shall love your neighbor as yourself.' There is no other commandment greater than these."

Affirm that Jesus is God and is the Only Way of Salvation. Salvation is not possible by obedience in Judaism, not through Mohammed's revelation of Allah (Islam), not through Buddhism or Hinduism, not by good works, and not through Jehovah's Witnesses or Mormonism. Salvation is only available through Jesus.

- John 14:6 "Jesus said to him, 'I am the way, and the truth, and the life. No one comes to the Father except through me.'"

- Acts 4:12 "And there is salvation in no one else, for there is no other name under heaven given among men by which we must be saved."

- 1 John 2:23 "No one who denies the Son has the Father. Whoever confesses the Son has the Father also."

4. Call out to Jesus in prayer to be in charge of your life

Publicly place your trust and faith in Him.

- Acts 16:30-31 Then he brought them out and said, "Sirs, what must I do to be saved?" [31] And they said, "Believe in the Lord Jesus, and you will be saved, you and your household."

- Romans 10:9-10 "if you confess with your mouth that Jesus is Lord and believe in your heart that God raised him from the dead, you will be saved. [10] For with the heart one believes and is justified, and with the mouth one confesses and is saved."
- Romans 10:13 "For 'everyone who calls on the name of the Lord will be saved.'"

Submit and yield to His Lordship. Let Him be in control of your life.

- Acts 2:37-38 "Now when they heard this they were cut to the heart, and said to Peter and the rest of the apostles, 'Brothers, what shall we do?' [38] And Peter said to them, "Repent and be baptized every one of you in the name of Jesus Christ for the forgiveness of your sins, and you will receive the gift of the Holy Spirit.
- Matthew 16:24-26 "Then Jesus told his disciples, 'If anyone would come after me, let him deny himself and take up his cross and follow me. [25] For whoever would save his life(1) will lose it, but whoever loses his life for my sake will find it. [26] For what will it profit a man if he gains the whole world and forfeits his soul? Or what shall a man give in return for his soul?'"

Now What? If you have chosen to believe that Jesus Christ is God, died on the cross, and rose from the grave and have truly yielded control of your life to Him, you are a Christian and follower of Jesus. *Here is what to do next...*

Walk with Jesus in Fellowship with Other Believers
Proclaim Christ's Lordship over your life through Baptism
- Acts 2:38 "And Peter said to them, 'Repent and be baptized every one of you in the name of Jesus Christ for the forgiveness of your sins, and you will receive the gift of the Holy Spirit.'"

See "What does the Bible say about Baptism?" on Trustworthy-Word.com
- www.trustworthyword.com/what-does-the-bible-say-about-baptism

Read your Bible to grow in your knowledge and love of Christ

See "How to Study the Bible?" on TrustworthyWord.com
- www.trustworthyword.com/how-to-study-the-bible

Pray consistently and daily to relate more with Jesus

See "What Does the Bible Say God is Like?" and "What Does the Bible Say about Christian Identity?" on Trustworthy-Word.com
- www.trustworthyword.com/what-does-the-bible-say-god-is-like
- www.trustworthyword.com/what-does-the-bible-say-about-christian-identity

Connect with a biblically faithful church family
- Hebrews 10:25-26 "And let us consider how to stir up one another to love and good works, 25 not neglecting to meet together, as is the habit of some, but encouraging one another, and all the more as you see the Day drawing near."

See "What Does the Bible Say about Church Membership?" on TrustworthyWord.com
- www.trustworthyword.com/what-does-the-bible-say-about-church-membership

Speak and Demonstrate God's Love
- Ephesians 2:10 "For we are his workmanship, created in Christ Jesus for good works, which God prepared beforehand, that we should walk in them."

See "What Does the Bible Say about Love?" on Trustworthy-Word.com
- www.trustworthyword.com/what-does-the-bible-say-about-love

Listen to and Obey God's Commands
- Hebrews 10:26-27 "For if we go on sinning deliberately after receiving the knowledge of the truth, there no longer remains a sacrifice for sins, 27 but a fearful expectation of judgment, and a fury of fire that will consume the adversaries."
- 1 Peter 1:15-16 "but as he who called you is holy, you also be holy in all your conduct, 16 since it is written, 'You shall be holy, for I am holy.'"

See "What Does the Bible Say about Sin?" and "What Does the Bible Say about Sanctification?" on TrustworthyWord.com
- www.trustworthyword.com/what-does-the-bible-say-about-sin
- www.trustworthyword.com/what-does-the-bible-say-about-sanctification

Common Objections to the Gospel

1. What about people who've never heard about Jesus? Will they go to Hell?

What about other religions: Muslims, Buddhists, Hindus, and tribal religions? A person doesn't go to Hell for failing to hear the Gospel, they go to hell for failing to obey God's law. Consider if a man jumped out of a plane without a parachute. He doesn't die primarily because he doesn't have a parachute. The reason he dies is because he violates the law of gravity...which brings him to his death. If a person dies without Christ, it is because he has transgressed the law of God... ignorance is not excuse. If we really care about those who have not heard about Jesus, we need to first come to Christ, and take His name, the only name which offers hope of salvation....to the ends of the earth.

2. My god is a god of love and forgiveness who doesn't send someone to hell.

This is an example of idolatry...a violation of the 2nd commandment. Crafting a god of our own imagination, in our own image, or a god we are comfortable with. We cannot separate God's justice from God's love. He does judge the wicked and the immoral by their transgression of the law, and their sentence is eternal death and suffering in a very real Hell. This same God, we learn from Romans 5:8, loved us so much, that while we were still rebels and enemies, sent His son to die for us.

3. Why is there so much suffering?

We all go through suffering. All of us have been hurt by the sinfulness of others, the consequences of living in a fallen world, and by our own sinfulness. We need to have faith in God, knowing and trusting that He is in control, and that His good plan includes an eternal rescue from sin, suffering, and death. It is good to ask these deep questions. I would recommend **www.gotquestions.org** to dig deeply into this question and other similarly tough questions. Ultimately God sent this message here today to help save you from eternal suffering. This is God's love.

4. I'm already saved.

God tells us to test ourselves to see if we are in the faith. Have our lives changed? Do we desire to hear God's voice through the Bible? Are we obedient to God's commands? Do we see the fruits of God's Spirit (love, joy, peace, patience, kindness, goodness, faithfulness, gentleness, self-control) in our lives? (Galatians 5:22-24) Or do we see the works of the flesh in our lives (sexual immorality, impurity, sensuality, idolatry, sorcery, enmity, strife, jealousy, fits of anger, rivalries, dissensions, divisions, envy, drunkenness, orgies, and things like these)? (Galatians 5:19-21) Do we desperately seek Him in prayer? Do we see righteousness being produced by God in our lives? Are we quick to forgive? Do we love others?

SEE "How Can I Be Sure I Am a Christian?" (the next chapter) or on TrustworthyWord.com @

- www.trustworthyword.com/how-can-i-be-sure-im-a-christian

When you see a doctor and you are sick, what does he do? He assess the symptoms, shoots straight with you, and tells you about your disease and any possible cures. The Bible clearly speaks to any symptoms of ongoing, unrepentant sin in our lives. Matthew 7:21 "I never knew you." Test yourselves.

5. I don't believe in God.

Just because we don't believe something doesn't make it disappear. Put on a blindfold and stand in front of a large truck on a highway, saying I don't believe the truck exists. I know there is no such thing as an atheist. No such thing as an atheist at 25,000 ft in crazy turbulence. Look at a painting, do you say, look what coincidentally formed by chance over a ridiculously long period of time? No. You see a painting. You know there is a painter. You see a building, you know there is a builder. You see the Creation and you know there is a Creator.

6. I don't believe the Bible is God's Word.

You are right the Bible was written by men. When you write a letter, do you write, or does the pen? Men are God's instruments to write the Bible. The Bible is the most accurate piece of literature in all of history...scientifically, historically, prophetically, archaeologically, and documentary or manuscript evidence. Find an error. We've searched. We can't find any.

7. I confess my sins and say I'm sorry all the time.

Consider civil law. If someone is guilty of a serious crime, when they come to trial, if they just say "I'm sorry" to the judge, do you think he'll just let her go? That's not fair. Only a corrupt or unrighteous judge would let a guilty person free without a penalty. The law has been broken. Justice demands a punishment. We can't just say we are sorry. We can't be "good enough" to overcome our crimes. We need Jesus to pay for the penalty for our sin.

8. I've lied, but that doesn't make me a bad person.

On moral issues...it only takes one commission of a crime to be labeled a criminal. One murder = a murderer. One lie = liar. One theft = a thief. One lust = adulterer. It is human nature to trivialize sin, but sin is serious. God tells us in James 2:10 that anyone who is guilty of one sin is guilty of all sin.

9. Christianity is narrow-minded.

The Bible is clear that there is only one way. Jesus says in John 14:6, "I am the way and the truth and the life, no one comes to the Father except through me." In Acts 4:12 we learn that there is only one "name under heaven given among men by which we must be saved." I you don't have the Son, don't have the Father. You're right, without Jesus, no hope for your transgression of the law. Jesus has the power to forgive sins... He openly offers that exclusive path to salvation to all who hear...would you reject Him? Put your faith in Him?

10. I don't agree with you.

No one knows when they will face death. Did you know that 150,000 people die every 24 hours? That is not a scare tactic, that is reality. And after death there is guaranteed judgment. Jesus speaks of the rich man and Lazarus, the rich man who is in Hell becomes desperate to tell his family about Jesus. Read Romans 2:4 – We plead with you to realize you are storing up wrath for yourself for the day of judgment...don't presume upon God's patience and kindness. Get right with the Lord. Consider our motives...we just want you to know and love Jesus and find eternal life. Paul in Romans 9 explains that he wishes he could sacrifice his own salvation for the salvation of someone else...but it doesn't work that way. You must decide.

THE BOTTOM LINE? There is no good objection for failing to follow Christ as your Lord. Do you have a good reason for putting Him off any longer?

Check out these resources for more answers!

- needgod.com
- gotquestions.org

HOW CAN I BE SURE I AM A CHRISTIAN?

WWW.CATHOLIC.BLOG/CHRISTIAN-BE-SURE

"Examine yourselves, to see whether you are in the faith. Test yourselves. Or do you not realize this about yourselves, that Jesus Christ is in you?— unless indeed you fail to meet the test!" 2 Corinthians 13:5 (ESV)

1. Did a work start in you?

· if you confess with your mouth that Jesus is Lord and believe in your heart that God raised him from the dead, you will be saved. (Romans 10:9)

· And I am sure of this, that he who began a good work in you will bring it to completion at the day of Jesus Christ. (Philippians 1:6)

2. Have you experienced God's Spirit in you?

· In him you also, when you heard the word of truth, the gospel of your salvation, and believed in him, were sealed with the promised Holy Spirit, who is the guarantee of our inheritance until we acquire possession of it, to the praise of his glory. (Ephesians 1:13-14)

3. Is there fruit of God's Spirit growing in you?
(Read the book of 1 John)

1. Do you enjoy having fellowship w/Christ & Christians? (1 John

1:3)

2. Would people say you walk in the light or darkness? (1 John 1:6-7)

3. Do you admit and confess your sin? (1 John 1:8)

4. Are you obedient to God's Word? (1 John 2:3-5)

5. Does your life indicate you love God or the world? (1 John 2:15)

6. Is your life characterized by "doing what is right"? (1 John 2:29)

7. Do you seek to maintain a pure life? (1 John 3:3)

8. Do you see a decreasing pattern of sin in your life? (1 John 3:5-6) [i.e. not continuing in sin as a way of life, not a total absence of sin.]

9. Do you demonstrate love for other Christians? (1 John 3:14)

10. Do you "walk the walk," vs just "talking the talk"? (1Jn 3:18-19)

11. Do you maintain a clear conscience? (1 John 3:21)

12. Do you experience victory in your Christian walk? (1 John 5:4)

4. Do you endure in the faith?
· They went out from us, but they were not of us; for if they had been of us, they would have continued with us. But they went out, that it might become plain that they all are not of us. (1 John 2:19)

Works of the Flesh vs. Fruits of the Spirit: What best describes you?
The "works of the flesh" are evidence for unbelief

and an eternity in Hell.

*The "fruit of the Spirit" evidences God's saving work
and eternity with Christ.* (Galatians 5:16-24)

[19] Now the works of the flesh are evident: sexual immorality, impurity, sensuality, [20] idolatry, sorcery, enmity, strife, jealousy, fits of anger, rivalries, dissensions, divisions, [21] envy, drunkenness, orgies, and things like these. I warn you, as I warned you before, that those who do such things will not inherit the kingdom of God.

[22] But the fruit of the Spirit is love, joy, peace, patience, kindness, goodness, faithfulness, [23] gentleness, self-control; against such things there is no law. [24] And those who belong to Christ Jesus have crucified the flesh with its passions and desires.

Parable of the Sower:
What category of "soil" best describes your
response to the good news about Jesus?
(Matthew 13:19-23 ESV)

1. [19] When anyone hears the word of the kingdom and does not understand it, the evil one comes and snatches away what has been sown in his heart. This is what was sown along the path.

2. [20] As for what was sown on rocky ground, this is the one who hears the word and immediately receives it with joy, [21] yet he has no root in himself, but endures for a while, and when tribulation or persecution arises on account of the word, immediately he falls away.

3. [22] As for what was sown among thorns, this is the one who hears the word, but the cares of the world and the deceitfulness of riches choke the word, and it proves unfruitful.

Only the fourth ("good") soil below describes a genuine Christian.

4. [23] As for what was sown on good soil, this is the one who hears the word and understands it. He indeed bears fruit and yields, in one case a hundredfold, in another sixty, and in another thirty.

Do You See These Three Characteristics in Your Life?
The Book of 1 John Helps Us to See Characteristics of Truly Converted and Saved Souls.

"I write these things to you who believe in the name of the Son of God that you may know that you have eternal life." (1 John 5:13)

1. Obedience to God's Commands?
- If we say we have fellowship with him while we walk in darkness, we lie and do not practice the truth. (1 John 1:6)
- Whoever says "I know him" but does not keep his commandments is a liar, and the truth is not in him, but whoever keeps his word, in him truly the love of God is perfected. By this we may know that we are in him: whoever says he abides in him ought to walk in the same way in which he walked. (1 John 2:4-6)
- If one turns away his ear from hearing the law, even his prayer is an abomination. (Proverbs 28:9)
- No one who abides in him keeps on sinning; no one who keeps on sinning has either seen him or known him. (1 John 3:6)
- By this it is evident who are the children of God, and who are the children of the devil: whoever does not practice righteousness is not of God, nor is the one who does not love his brother. (1 John 3:10)
- For this is the love of God, that we keep his commandments. And his commandments are not burdensome. (1 John 5:3)

2. Forgiveness?

- Whoever says he is in the light and hates his brother is still in darkness. (1 John 2:9)
- For if you forgive others their trespasses, your heavenly Father will also forgive you, but if you do not forgive others their trespasses, neither will your Father forgive your trespasses. (Matt 6:14-15)

3. Love?

- If anyone loves the world, the love of the Father is not in him. (1 John 2:15)
- No one who denies the Son has the Father. (1 John 2:23)
- But if anyone does not provide for his relatives, and especially for members of his household, he has denied the faith and is worse than an unbeliever. (1 Timothy 5:8)
- Anyone who does not love does not know God, because God is love. (1 John 4:8)

ABOUT THE AUTHOR

Dr. Jonathan Carl

After growing up in the great state of Texas, Jonathan found himself in Kentucky after marrying his wonderful wife Brittney. Several years later he became the lead pastor at South Fork Baptist Church where he now serves. After graduating from the United States Military Academy at West Point, Jonathan served in the U.S. Army as a tanker and completed a tour in Iraq in the early 2000s. He earned his Master of Divinity and Doctor of Philosophy degree in Evangelism & Missions from the Southern Baptist Theological Seminary. Jonathan & Brittney have four daughters (Sophia, Lydia, Alia & Mia) with whom they enjoy spending every spare minute they can.

Please check out www.Catholic.blog or www.TrustworthyWord.com for more free print and video Bible study resources from Jonathan!

Titus 1:9 "He must hold firm to the trustworthy word as taught, so that he may be able to give instruction in sound doctrine and also to rebuke those who contradict it." (ESV)